Feast

Feast

Poetry & Recipes for a Full Seating at Dinner

Edited by Diane Goettel and Anneli Matheson

With an introduction by Susanne Paola Antonetta

Black
Lawrence
Press

www.blacklawrence.com

Executive Editor: Diane Goettel
Book and cover design: Amy Freels

Published 2015 by Black Lawrence Press.
Printed in the United States.

Foreword

This book, like a great meal, has been a labor of love.

We are delighted to serve up *Feast: Poetry & Recipes for a Full Seating at Dinner*—a scrumptious offering for the mind and body that is both a poetry anthology and a cookbook.

Over the years at Black Lawrence Press our senses have been captivated by an abundance of food-inspired poetry in the many collections we have published. And our poet friends are not only writing about food but also cooking it up and sharing their photos and recipes all over social media. Frankly, they have left us salivating and wanting more for far too long now—and not just wanting more words but more *food*. We're ready for a feast!

Lest we expire in this state of constant temptation and hunger, we decided to curate a genre-fusion work of art around a dinner party theme, and thus *Feast: Poetry & Recipes for a Full Seating at Dinner* was born. This book you hold in your hands is full of beautiful language, words and images, absolutely; but it's also about the preparation, cooking and sharing of food—which is ultimately about relationships, shared memories, taking risks and getting messy.

It's an exciting time to be a home cook. What was once the mysterious domain of elite chefs has become the stomping ground for anyone willing to roll up their sleeves and learn. Fiery flambés, soft soufflés, and rich risottos can be found sizzling, rising, and simmering in kitchens across the country. While a few of our poet contributors have been to culinary school and written their own cookbooks, the majority are accomplished home cooks who have specifically created and tested, or uniquely adapted, the recipes that compliment their poems.

Feast is structured like a classic cookbook, moving from drinks and appetizers to main courses and dessert. The poems are inspired by the spirit of the toast, that lovely old fashioned public declaration to invoke celebration, express gratitude, or acknowledge a loss. As you read through *Feast*, you will join a dinner party in progress. To name a few of the sweet and savory delights you now hold in your hands, consider: Juditha Dowd calls attention to citrus and lingering conversation shared over an orange, onion and watercress salad. Ruth Bavetta brings a fine catch of the sea, moonlight and Norwegian sardines to the table. Daniel Olivas introduces his friend Georgina, who is very particular about two things, and reveals the only way to make a margarita. Lynn Hoffman pours homebrewed beer in Eddy's kitchen with a toast to Buster. Joe Wilkins mixes up white sangria with lights from a streetlamp to drink with a supper both animal and sacred. Michele Battiste cooks cabbage noodles and considers when the cabbage is not just a vegetable but something much more complicated. Daniele Pantano chops and dices ingredients for tomato sauce and swears never to wear his father's mask. Eric Morris prepares pork spare ribs and offers a toast to animals slaughtered and yams candied. Arnold Johnston remembers once upon a distant New Year's Eve as Scottish shortbread rises in the oven. Dolores Stewart Riccio spins a blue story of a sculptor to serve alongside fresh blueberry tea cake. Please consider sharing these poems aloud to begin or end your meal.

Lord Byron wrote, in *The Island*, "Since Eve ate apples, much depends on dinner." We believe that much still does. Writing, like cooking, is difficult work. Hospitality, like writing, is personal and risky. Whenever we invite someone to read our creative work or into our home to share a meal, we create the possibility for friendship as well as disaster. Our daily bread of stress, deadlines, to-do lists and ubiquitous technology make it easy to retreat in exhaustion and avoid the inconvenience of hosting.

As writers we must persevere with the craft and discipline of poetry-making because we trust it's worth the time and effort. As people we must protect and cultivate our relationships, even when the act of caring intrudes upon our word work. This book is an invitation to feast on rich poems stuffed with delectable words, while also chowing down with friends at a homemade dinner party. Think about sage gin fizzes and vegetarian stuffed artichokes, followed by pot roast, soda bread and coconut squash soup, with a grand finale of bananas foster and chocolate fondant. Prepare whatever sparks your imagination—what matters is that the meal is shared.

Tantalized?

We thought so.

Before we start reading and cooking we want to conclude with a toast of our own: May *Feast*, both its words and recipes, inspire many a nourishing gathering among friends and family both new and old. May there be thought-provoking words, ambrosial aromas, yummy bites and toothsome conversations. After all, much depends on the dinner you choose to have, and the company you choose to share it with.

Feast well, friends!

Anneli & Diane

Artful Eating

An Introduction to Feast: Poetry & Recipes for a Full Seating at Dinner

Susanne Paola Antonetta

In *Twelfth Night*, Shakespeare has Duke Orsino begin the play with one of literature's most famous invitations: "If music be the food of love, play on." Music is what the "musicians attending" play for lovesick Orsino, and also what the playwright in his verse provides for us, the audience. The music of poetry serves as "the food of love," and it is a music we the audience must also bid "play on" as the story's love plots unfold. The poet's words, artfully arranged, can, like Orsino's musicians, provide us with love's nutriment. Poetry feeds us, and it feeds our loves.

Poetry is music (and in fact, functional MRIs performed at the University of Exeter in England show that poetry stimulates the same part of our brain that music does), and poetry, like music, is essential to the feast. Can we even tell music, abundance, and poetry apart? In these pages, Dolores Stewart Riccio, in her "How to Make a Tomato Salad," describes the fruit as "juicy and full of seeds, a woman ripe for love." And who can resist the physicality of Natasha Saje's invitation to a pear Napoleon, and perhaps, much more—the phyllo pastry "between whose sheets I'll slip / toasted, slivered, blanched almonds. / I'll cut the pastry into hearts," and all of this goodness "in the hot oven waiting."

Of course, poetry, like food, can give us one of love's best physical equivalencies, a rush of sensory pleasure. And poetry can do far more: issue invitations; whet our appetites; provide toasts that focus a meal on its larger human meaning (a wedding, a birthday, a death); lament what is gone; and celebrate a world that gives us such things as plums, and melons, and even wine. Recall here how wine diverted John Keats even from the marvels of the nightingale, highjacking a ten-line stanza in "Ode to a Nightingale" from that "immortal Bird," with its seductive "beaded bubbles winking at the brim."

As long as poetry has existed, it has embraced the subject of the table. "The Salad," attributed to Roman poet Virgil, describes the creation of a cheese and garlic paste that bears a strong resemblance to today's pesto. In the 1600s, Japanese poet Basho wrote a haiku that did for melons what William Carlos Williams' short poem "This Is Just to Say" did for plums: the "coolness of the melons / flecked with mud" reaching across time and oceans to embrace Williams' plums: "delicious / so sweet / and so cold."

In fact, many meals have not been considered complete without a poetic accompaniment, from the chanting of Robert Burns' "Ode to a Haggis" for a haggis dinner in Scotland to the wedding prayer-poems of the native peoples of the Great Plains. The feast—with all the delights of the mead halls—was a mainstay of Anglo-Saxon poetry; at the table, so full of "rare dishes of the richest foods" that the table itself disappeared beneath them, Sir Gawain fatefully encountered the Green Knight.

No less a source than the classic *Physiology of Taste, or Transcendental Gastronomy*, written by Jean Anthelme Brillat-Savarin in the early 1800s, mentions poetry multiple times, and stresses the historic importance of poetry to the great meal: "At that time [of the writing of the *Odyssey*] and long before, beyond doubt, poetry and music were mingled with meals. Famous minstrels sang the wonders of nature, the loves of the gods, and warlike deeds of man," wrote the father of modern gastronomy.

Intertwined in the poetry of physicality is the physicality of poetry. Poets recognize this quality of poetry intuitively—that it calls out to our senses in a special way among the literary arts—and strive to put language to the way poetry affects our bodies. Emily Dickinson wrote in a letter to Thomas Wentworth Higginson, "If I read a book and it makes my whole body so cold no fire can warm me I know that is poetry. If I feel physically as if the top of my head were taken off, I know that is poetry. These are the only way I know it. Is there any other way?" (If Dickinson had had this book in her hand, she might have added, "If I feel physically as if I must get up and make a Waldorf salad, I know *that* is poetry.")

French poet Paul Valéry distinguished between prose and poetry by calling prose the form that readers respond to "only in spirit," whereas he declared poetry the form that calls forth an inner physical response in the reader to a poem's world, one which involves the body in "more of a complete act." Therefore, in Valéry's thinking, Amy Lee Scott's poem "The Best Meal in the World Began . . ." is more than an artful arrangement of words; it is the inner savor of the pomegranate, the crisp sweetness of the dacquoise.

Feast: Poetry & Recipes for a Full Seating at Dinner is divided into four sections: "Starters, Sides and Sauces"; "Cocktails"; "Mains"; "Dessert." As even the pleasure of dining alone evokes the possible community of the table, these poems bring people to life along with their dishes—the poet Yelizaveta P. Renfro's mother, for instance, in "Here's to My Mother Making Herring Under a Fur Coat" ("Here's to greenery, to garnish, to the striped seeds she placed in a cellophane envelope and brought with her to America" —Renfro's long lines can barely contain her mother's exuberant spirit).

Some poems in this collection, like Eric Morris's "Drink to the Animals" and John J. Trause's "Cheers on the Cobblestones," are lusty toasts; others, like Claire Van Winkle's "Kitchen Histories," have a note of elegy, of meals that, in their transience, might imply the transience of those who served them.

Some of these feasting poems celebrate those whom we love to nourish, and who nourish us. Robert Avery in "In Praise of Consumable Art" celebrates his spouse's creation of "another fine / confection only the two of us will know," and Emily Bright in "At the End of a Busy Day" confesses "I have prepared this food for you. / There were other things I had to do." Other poems, like Joe Wilkins's "Eat Stone and Go On," explore the scarcities of the table, the "burnt chuck" over which his grandmother said, "Isn't it a shame . . . / how we have to go on eating?"

Of course, this book is only partly—though delightfully!—about the poems. (And perhaps if she'd caught a look at some of these recipes, Joe Wilkins's grandmother might have perked up about the routine of eating.) Robert Avery's example of "consumable art" happens to be a luxurious dessert tart composed of chocolate, raspberries, Chambord, butter and cream. We can't indulge in such artworks every day, so we also have breads, fritters, a squash soup with coconut milk, pastas aswim in sauces simmered from ripe, fresh tomatoes. There are recipes to suit every skill level: from simple salads and quick meals like steamed mussels to a "revisionist" Caprese salad—actually a dessert—featuring basil ice cream and tomato "rocks" that will challenge those who treasure time spent preparing the unique and the wonderful in the kitchen.

"Animals feed themselves," wrote Brillat-Savarin, "men eat, but only wise men know the art of eating." How much wiser, then, are we who know the art of eating with poetry. And if poets are intrinsic to the feast, then how much more special the feast where the dishes—and the words—are poet-provided?

Elizabethan poet Ben Jonson wrote, in the poem "Inviting a Friend to Supper," one of literature's most charming poetic calls to dine:

> Tonight, grave sir, both my poor house, and I
> Do equally desire your company;
> Not that we think us worthy such a guest,
> But that your worth will dignify our feast . . .
> Yet shall you have, to rectify your palate,
> An olive, capers, or some better salad
> Ushering the mutton; with a short-legged hen,

If we can get her, full of eggs, and then
Lemons, and wine for sauce; to these a cony[1]
Is not to be despaired of, for our money;
And, though fowl now be scarce, yet there are clerks,
The sky not falling, think we may have larks.
I'll tell you of more, and lie, so you will come:
Of partridge, pheasant, woodcock, of which some
May yet be there, and godwit, if we can;
Knat, rail, and ruff[2] too. Howsoe'er, my man
Shall read a piece of Virgil, Tacitus,
Livy, or of some better book to us,
Of which we'll speak our minds, amidst our meat;
And I'll profess no verses to repeat.

It is a poet's invitation, complete with poems read aloud (including plenty of warlike deeds and loves of the gods; Brillat-Savarin would approve), larks, wine, and a refusal to promise not to lie. Like their forebear Jonson, these poets invite you to their table. And like Jonson, they can only promise to speak their minds, and repeat no verses. Do come in and enjoy the pleasures of the table.

---

1. rabbit
2. "knat, rail, and ruff" describes an edible English fowl

Starters, Sides & Sauces

Cocktails

Mains

Dessert

Starters, Sides & Sauces

"The poets have been mysteriously silent on the subject of cheese."
—GK Chesterton

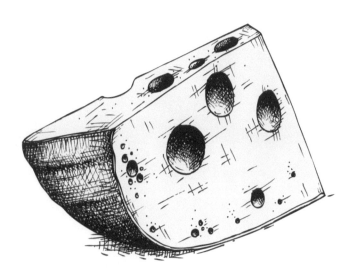

Ode to Sardines

Ruth Bavetta

The northern sea,
immaculate and immense,
drops anchor
on my kitchen counter.
Moonlight reassembled
as layers of watered silk
head to tail
in a bright tin coffin.

Sardiner Med Senap

(Sardines with Mustard, a Norwegian recipe)

Ruth Bavetta

Ingredients

Siljans Knekkebrod (crispbread)—2 large rings
3 cans King Oscar Tiny Tots sardines
Pickled onion slices
Dijon mustard

Instructions

Break crisp bread into irregular pieces and spread with mustard. Top with sardines and onion slices.

Take Two

Loretta Oleck

salute!
to being here before
back in the hollow of my life
where I box-stepped with hungry ghosts
where dinner was dimmer-

a white of an egg
a chilled Chablis
a frantic search through
the spice rack to find a jar
of crushed red pepper-

anything, and I mean *anything*
to add a punch to the flatness
and the dead

salute!
to sitting at the same lopsided table
the same corner seat from that other life
ordering mussels served in a silver pot
watching my night unfold like a Spanish fan
snapped open with a flick of a wrist

god, I never knew there were dots of gold
curls of sea green on the fluttering fan
cooling down the flush across my cheeks

pressing my back against the brilliant red
lipstick walls cloaking me in a warm wanting
dream where day becomes night

I lick the tip of each finger
tracing my lips with pink salt and parsley
scooping up a mussel
slurping out the meat
drinking down the garlic broth

I didn't understand, no I really *didn't*
understand how much I love
sucking on mussel shells
in this out of the way place
I've been to before

salute!
to a new life opening
revealing itself
in a most flavorful broth

Mussels with Parsley and Garlic

Loretta Oleck

Ingredients

6 tablespoons unsalted butter, divided
⅓ cup finely chopped shallot
4 garlic cloves, minced
¼ teaspoon dried hot red pepper flakes (adjust to suit your taste)
1 cup chicken or vegetable broth
¾ cup water
2 pounds mussels (preferably cultivated), scrubbed well and
　beards removed
3 tablespoons chopped fresh parsley
Salt and pepper to taste

Instructions

Cook the shallot, garlic, and red pepper flakes in 2 tablespoons oil in a large skillet over moderate heat, stirring until softened (about 2–3 minutes). Add the broth and water; bring to a simmer. Add the mussels and cook covered, over moderately high heat until they open wide, checking frequently after 3–4 minutes. Transfer the opened mussels to a bowl. Any mussels that remain unopened after about eight minutes total should be discarded.

Stir in parsley. Whisk remaining butter, one tablespoon at a time, into the mussel broth and season with salt and pepper.

Divide mussels and broth among six to ten bowls.
Garnish with bread that you can be used to dip into the broth, and serve.

Serves 6—10

Here's to My Mother Making Herring Under a Fur Coat

Yelizaveta P. Renfro

Here's to greenery, to garnish, to the striped seeds she placed in a
cellophane envelope and brought with her to America, to the waist-high
dill plants gone to flower that conquered our California yard—

(And here's to mayonnaise, and Soviet lines, to scarcity and shortages,
to "What's the line for?" said gruffly, in the Russian way, and the
answers: sausage, shoes, cheese, and one day, mayonnaise—)

And to beets, bleeding out their savage purple on counters, staining
fingers, adding a dash of haute couture to the herring's coat, or at least
pizzazz, or at least a luminous borscht glow, and to the five-year-old
who once told me she loved beets because they taste like purple mud—

(And to mayonnaise again, because the line was long, and sometimes
Soviet lines didn't move for hours, and sometimes the supply ran out
long before demand was satisfied, so you never knew if you were going
to get anything, and sometimes, it seemed, the weary Soviets didn't even
bother to ask what a line was for, because if there's a line, there must be
something good at the end of it, or at least the hope of something good,
so standing in line gave them more than anything else could at that
moment, and the line, if you stood in it long enough, became a life form
of its own, a multi-segmented creature that flexed and angered and shed
and, when all hope was lost, disintegrated—and all of this that day in
1987 waiting to buy mayonnaise—)

And here's to eggs, to their ovoid perfection at the bazaar, but now you wonder—however did they get carried home? Perhaps they were cradled gently against the hollows of the body in buses chockablock with people, just like the day your mother stood in line to acquire a new butcher knife, wrapped only in coarse brown paper, and she curled herself around it on the teeming bus, cradling it like an infant, fearful of eviscerating one of the bodies jammed against her—such is the care we take with that which is fragile, that which is dangerous—

(And mayonnaise: you stood in line for two hours, but since you were a tourist, collecting experiences, seeking exotica, you never grew defeated or weary; you always knew you had an out, a return to the land where mayonnaise jars gleamed from ceiling to floor like museum specimens, each with its own identifying label—)

And here's to carrots, and to the ancient crone outside the metro selling her lassoed bundles of carrots as crooked as her bent, arthritic fingers, perched on a shipwreck of a crate, wincing as she counted out kopecks in her burled hands—

(And oh, the mayonnaise: we lavish it on with a knife, like frosting, like something plentiful and delicious, because this is the Russian way—to spend days scouring the city, bartering, negotiating, so the final spread seems effortless, a quick laying out of a few things on hand, and never mind that the local store offers nothing but white vinegar and brown cakes of soap, the food is nothing at all, a trifle—)

To onion, because there are tears, always tears, and later, more tears with the vodka or the homemade currant wine, and talk of souls wrought with Dostoyevskian intensity, because Russians are as familiar with their souls as they are with their beet-stained fingers, and with the soul talk, more tears—

(And decades later, when she makes the salad in your kitchen, she will always use up nearly the entire jar, leaving only a smear around the sides, a clot in the bottom, and for months you'll be reminded by the marks she's left: a glimmering of beet along the rim, or a single purple thumbprint on the Hellman's label—)

And here's to potatoes, because if you have potatoes, she always intones, you will never starve, and here's to digging the new potatoes in the earth of the dacha, some hardly larger than peas, and though you are only nine years old, you recognize that this has never happened to you before and will never happen to you again: digging potatoes with your Russian grandfather, who was born in czarist times, whose own mother was an illiterate peasant, and whose forbears were serfs—

(And mayonnaise again, because when you ask for the recipe, she sends you a mere list of the layers in order, with no quantities, no directions, save one: "The mayonnaise must be used in between.")

And finally, here's to herring, which your mother still demands come directly from a wooden barrel, though she'll settle, when necessary, for the jarred fillets, because that's what Russians do, they settle for what's at hand, and she's settled for a lot in America—but here's to America anyway, and here's to the labor of each layer, to queues and digging and roubles, to rolled Russian R's, but more than that, here's to the layers of the past, to the thick deposits of nostalgia, slathered on, glomming it all together.

Herring Under a Fur Coat

(Russian Salad)

Yelizaveta P. Renfro

Ingredients

3 medium beets

4 eggs

4 carrots

3 medium potatoes

1 medium onion

2 cups mayonnaise

12 ounces of salted or pickled herring

Sprigs of fresh dill or parsley

Instructions

Place the beets, eggs, carrots, and potatoes in a pan of water and boil until cooked through. After cooling, peel the beets, eggs, carrots, and potatoes, and then coarsely grate them, placing them in separate bowls. Grate the onion, and dice the herring. Now you are ready to assemble the salad.

In a large, glass bowl, place the ingredients in the following order, creating layers: herring on the bottom, followed by ⅓ cup of mayonnaise, then potato, ⅓ cup mayonnaise, onion, ⅓ cup mayonnaise, carrots, ⅓ cup mayonnaise, eggs, ⅓ cup mayonnaise, beets, topped with ⅓ cup mayonnaise. Once assembled, the salad should resemble a frosted torte. Garnish with dill or parsley. Refrigerate several hours before serving.

Serves 8–10

What Remains

Claire McQuerry

When one season is at the brink
        of spilling over, you recall
the way you walked, ankle-high
        in yellow leaves, a year ago,

or maybe two—
        it could have been two
months for all the lapse, except
        the light now, its bright tone

of between: the vibration
        that gathers before winter's coma.
A kaleidoscope of Novembers—
        where did you hear that time

is a thing like a crystal,
        the facets remaining unchanged
when it fractures ever smaller?
        Confirmation class. A vine

and leaf stitch rimmed the altar,
        the mantles green, for epiphany.
Here, lichen and helicon moth, sun
        caught in descent. *Teach us to number*

our days, the reverend had read—
        a hope that something is saved
in the contemplation, saved in your waking
        one morning to recall

the voice of wind in this burnt-out
        gully, branches black, arterial,
leaves fallen deep
        on the path over the ridge.

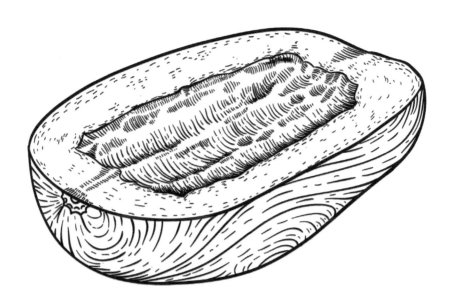

Fall Soup with Coconut Milk and Butternut Squash

Claire McQuerry

Ingredients

¾ cup low-sodium chicken broth

1½ tablespoon brown sugar

1 tablespoon salt

2 tablespoon tomato paste

1 teaspoon crushed red pepper

¼ tablespoon black pepper

1 (14 ounce) can coconut milk

2 cups butternut squash, peeled and cut into ¾ inch cubes

1 cup red bell pepper, cut into thin strips

1 pound raw, cubed chicken breast

2 cups hot cooked basmati rice

¼ cup fresh lime juice

3 tablespoons minced fresh cilantro

Instructions

Combine chicken broth and next 6 ingredients (through coconut milk) in a large saucepan and stir with a whisk.

Stir in squash and bell peppers and bring to a boil. Add chicken. Reduce heat and simmer for about 10 minutes or until squash is tender and chicken is cooked through.

Stir in rice, lime juice, and cilantro. Heat for 2 minutes.

Serves 6

Eat Stone and Go On

Joe Wilkins

Isn't it a shame, my grandmother said,
silver fork in her shivering fist,

how we have to go on eating?
We were sitting up to burnt chuck,

potatoes in their dirty jackets,
and hunks of Irish brown bread,

the two of us sitting up at the old wood table,
the one years ago my grandfather built

of planks pulled from an abandoned mine.
My grandmother stared at her plate.

She couldn't have been
more than a hundred pounds then,

the palsy at work in her hands,
her hung face. I was fifteen and hungry.

I had shoveled for her that day
two tons of furnace coal.

It was nearly winter. The summer past,
my grandfather had gone ahead

and died. Even if it was only
soda bread and fried steaks, I see now

it was something. I shoveled
another forkful of buttered potato

into my mouth, bits of the stone
we call salt between my teeth.

Soda Bread

Joe Wilkins

Ingredients

2 cups stone-ground whole-wheat flour

⅓ cup wheat bran

¼ cup toasted wheat germ

2 cups unbleached white flour

½ teaspoon salt

1 tablespoon baking powder

¼ teaspoon baking soda

⅓ cup sugar

1 tablespoon sour cream

1 large egg

1 ½ cups buttermilk

1 cup milk

Instructions

Preheat oven to 350° Fahrenheit. Butter two 9-by-5-by-3-inch pans.

In a large bowl, stir together the whole-wheat flour, bran, wheat germ, white flour, salt, baking powder, and baking soda. In another bowl, combine the sugar, sour cream, and eggs, and whisk well. Add the buttermilk and milk. Whisk again.

Make a well in the flour mixture, and pour the egg mixture into it. Stir well with a wooden spoon until the ingredients are incorporated. Pour the batter into the prepared pans. Bake for 50 minutes, or until a knife poked into the middle comes out clean.

Turn the bread out of the pan and let cool for 15 minutes. Serve with butter.

At the End of a Busy Day

Emily Bright

I have prepared this food for you.
There were other things I had to do
today—some of them quite urgent,
some routine and slow. What I meant
to say, in truth, was I chose you
this morning when I made the crust, you
when I sautéed. I was thinking this as
the day sped through with its crisis
and catastrophe-averted: even
if the food gets burnt, at seven
you'll arrive and place your shoes just there,
lift your fork and settle in your chair.

French Zucchini Tart

Emily Bright

Ingredients

Crust:
1 ½ cups flour
7 tablespoons butter
½ teaspoon salt
½ cup water

Filling:
2 large zucchini
3 medium onions
3 teaspoons of butter or oil
1 teaspoon salt
Pepper to taste
1 heaping tablespoon of flour
⅔ cup milk
½ cup grated gruyere cheese (can also use fresh parmesan)

Instructions

To prepare the crust, mix the flour and salt together in a bowl. Cut the butter into small pieces and mix it into the flour with either your fingers or a pastry cutter. Add cold water little by little and mix quickly. You may add slightly more water if necessary. Form the dough into a ball. Wrap it into plastic wrap and let it chill in the refrigerator for at least 30 minutes. Working on a lightly floured surface, roll the dough into a circle and press it into a 9 inch or 10 inch quiche pan.

Preheat oven to 400° Fahrenheit.

Slice the onions. In a large pan, heat the butter or oil. Add onions and cook until golden. Cut the zucchini into small cubes (½ inch) and add them to the onions. Stir until the cubes become transparent. Add salt, pepper, and flour. Stir. Add the milk while stirring. Let cook until it becomes thick and gluey. Remove from heat. Add cheese. Pour into pie crust. Cook 20–25 minutes or until top is golden.

Cheers on the Cobblestones

John J. Trause

Ortolan and octopus carpaccio, flaugnarde and clafoutis
champagne, prosecco, Sekt and Asti
cincin on the cobblestones *cincin*
saganaki, mavrodafni, ruby porto
fritto misto, queso fresco, yum, alfresco
aguardiente sin azucar, aguardiente sin azucar…
I toast to love, I toast to life,
I toast to you—*cincin*! *cincin*! *cent'anni*!

Cobblestone Cake

A Savory Appetizer

John J. Trause

Ingredients

15 cups of croutons (plain or lightly seasoned)
1 ½ pounds of Gruyère or Emmenthal cheese
1 tablespoon of powdered mustard seed
Butter
10 sprigs of fresh rosemary
2 whole lemons

Instructions

Lay the croutons in one layer on buttered cookie sheets into ten groups of 5 inch x 5 inch squares making sure that there are no gaps between the croutons.

Slice the cheese into very thin sheets and cover with one or two layers the top of the croutons, leaving no crouton uncovered.

Sprinkle ½ teaspoon of the mustard powder evenly over the cheese.

Bake in an oven pre-heated at 350° Fahrenheit until the cheese bubbles without burning.

Let the crouton squares cool for about ten minutes.

With a wide spatula lift up each crouton square and flip over onto its own dish, so that the croutons are on top, forming a cobblestone pattern.

Serve each cobblestone cake with a lemon wedge and a sprig of rosemary.

Serves 10

Conversing with an Orange

Juditha Dowd

Yüksel taught us the right way
to eat the Turkish *portakal*.
You do it slowly, talking with friends,
attentive to the task.

I saw that preparation
can be an aspect of taste,
as time may often be of place,
and I memorized the rule:

Slice off the stem,
work your knife in carefully
under the pebbled skin.
Score it in six vertical lines.

An orange can last all evening
with a glass of sweetened tea,
talk melding with the fruit,
the stacked elliptical peel.

You climb the honey-scented hills
of Izmir or Mersin,
build a small white fortress
from the wrinkled seeds.

Orange, Onion & Watercress Salad

Juditha Dowd

Ingredients

Salad:

4 large navel oranges

1 large, mild red onion

3 large bunches of watercress

Handful of small black olives, preferably Niçoise

Salt

1 recipe dressing, below

Dressing:

⅓ cup red wine vinegar

½ teaspoon salt

1 teaspoon Dijon mustard

½ cup cold-pressed olive oil

Black pepper to taste

Instructions

For the salad, peel the onion. Slice in thin rounds. Separate into rings and place them in a colander in the sink. Sprinkle rings with salt (about 1 tablespoon) and toss to distribute. Let stand for 20–30 minutes, then rinse very well and wrap onion rings in a dishtowel to dry. They should be slightly limp.

Wash watercress well, spin dry and trim off any tough stems or bruised leaves. Cut into small, attractive sprigs.

Pare oranges, removing all white pith. Slice in quarter inch rounds, removing seeds as you go and saving juice to add to the salad dressing. If the oranges are very large, cut the rounds in half.

For the dressing, whisk together vinegar, salt and mustard in a small bowl. Add any juices collected from preparing oranges. Slowly whisk in olive oil. Season well with black pepper.

The salad may be plated as individual servings for a first course but is attractive presented on a large white platter for guests to help themselves. Line the platter with watercress sprigs. Arrange orange slices in groups or lines over the watercress. Arrange onion slices over the oranges and scatter the black olives randomly. Pour dressing over salad, or pass at table in a small pitcher.

Serves 8

Fruit

Laura Madeline Wiseman

was crucial to the vegetarian diet—and despite my in-laws
meat and potatoes puzzlement—I devoured whole platters
of fresh pineapple, watermelon, cantaloupe, the way
large strawberries stained the lips red—who cares
if the diet was different. I was twenty-seven.
I'd just married my college sweetheart.
Heady from fructose, foreplay, and youth,
the heat of their small-town in September
and the triumph of my in-laws' bafflement.

I was forking muskmelon onto a paper plate,
sucking the pits from sweet cherries, wiping
my chin, only fruit and my groom to savor:
honeycrisps and Adam, golden delicious and pink ladies—
seeing the world through the spray of clementines—
all those cherry stems in knots, all that soft, warm flesh,
juice on my fingers, everywhere the spit seeds.

Fruit Platter

Laura Madeline Wiseman

Ingredients
pineapple
watermelon
muskmelon
cantaloupe
strawberries
cherries
other seasonal fruit, if desired

Instructions
Cube melons and pineapple. Arrange on platter. Serve.

Serves 6–8

How to Make a Tomato Salad

Dolores Stewart Riccio

The tomato
warm from the garden bed,
juicy and full of seeds, a woman ripe for love.

The onion,
make it sweet and lingering—
adulterous kisses, darkness at noon

Dashes of salt, a taste of the source,
the sea coming in the window.

A full blessing of oil—
the fruity olives pressed
by monks chanting *a cappella,*
the earthenware jugs stored in cool cellars,
mellowing.

The basil leaves, spicy and fragrant—
a lover's fingers.

You cannot make too much of this.
And when it's gone…

its memory will, in barren winter,
be like the small hot flame
of a love letter read in secret.

Tomato Salad

Dolores Stewart Riccio

Ingredients

6 medium vine-ripened tomatoes or 4 large (2 pounds total),
   sliced not quartered
1 Vidalia or other sweet onion, peeled and ringed
Salt to taste (cannot be omitted)
⅓ cup olive oil
6 to 8 fresh basil leaves, snipped
Fresh white Italian bread

Instructions

Put sliced tomatoes and onion rings in a flat vegetable serving dish. Sprinkle with salt. The salt encourages the tomatoes to exude juice. The slightly acidic tomato juice then replaces vinegar, combining with the oil into a mild vinaigrette.

Add the olive oil and basil. Stir gently with 2 forks. Let the salad stand at room temperature, stirring occasionally, for 30 minutes or so.

Serve with bread for dipping in the accumulated juices

Serves 4–6

The Artichoke

Vivian Shipley

Precisely what draws me to foods, to words
that must be cracked, pried open, puzzled apart?
The artichoke, for example, offers no tropical ease,
doesn't fulfill dreams of extending my hand
from a hammock to pluck mangos just to nibble
or lick, ignoring the juice on my chin, and flesh
clinging to hairy seeds. It must be the ratio of effort
to reward that lures me. To spend so much time
peeling off so many leaves for a piece of pale
green mush is an indulgence, say, like writing poems
that generate wastebaskets of paper for a few words.

Artichokes don't give themselves away to greed
or incompetence. They have to be approached slowly;
their quality of refusal must be listed to be understood:
complicated treasure-box; haughty, elegant courtesans
or rare peacocks whose feathers are not easily glimpsed.

Other foods such as oysters, crabs, pomegranates
and coconuts require a strategy. Few, however, lend
themselves to out and out revenge. Forced to house
and feed Germans in World War II, the French steamed
only enough artichokes for the troops in order to leave
the Nazis utterly at a loss. With no hosts to imitate,
the soldiers choked, chewed through every bristle, leaf

and thorn. Granted, it was a small act by a powerless
people, but satisfying as legumes can be, sprouting
to a pea that bruises, a bean that climbs to a castle.

Even fewer vegetables lend themselves to psychological
analysis, but I can tell a lot about a man by the way
he eats his artichoke, with leaves strewn about or stacked
in neat piles. Banished from the garden, cast out into
a forbidding world, I can locate delicacies in the most
unlikely places: juice of a prickly pear; truffles under
oaks, or meat of black walnuts, hard to crack, with husks
that stain white gloves. It's an artichoke, nonetheless,
that inspires me to write poems that explore poignancy,
woman's fall from Eden. Occasional but exquisite,
a taste of pure pleasure is compensation, but even dipped
in butter laced with lemon garlic or drizzled in olive oil,
what an effort it is to strip incisor widths of flesh from
the tips of leaves just to make it all the way to the heart.

Sicilian Artichokes

Vivian Shipley

Ingredients

8 small artichokes (trim stems, remove outer leaves and
  cut off 1 inch of top).

For the dip:
16 ounces of sour cream
2 packets of French onion dip
4 tablespoons minced green pepper
2 tablespoons minced red pepper
4 tablespoons of snipped fresh parsley
2 teaspoons lemon juice
1 teaspoon dried oregano
6 tablespoons whole milk

Instructions

Mix all ingredients for the dip together and chill.

Brush artichokes with lemon juice, then cook in boiling salted water
about 20 minutes until a leaf pulls out easily. Drain upside down and chill.

Serve artichokes with the dip. To eat, dip leaves in mix and draw
through teeth to eat only the tender flesh. With a fork, dip pieces of the
heart—minus the furry choke.

The History of the Radish

Marcela Sulak

In in its wild state it's utterly unknown,
but it may come from China or Japan
and may descend from *Raphanus Raphan-
istrum.* In days of Pharaohs, it was grown
extensively in Egypt. How its name,
from Saxon, *rude, rudo,* or *reod,*
or from the Sanskrit *rudhira,* for blood,
was hid from Britain till Gerard would claim
in 1597, four distinct
varieties. From cellophane, denude
of greeny tops, or peasant fingers, rude
and cakey earth, we lift them to the sink,
recalling how Egyptian women dyed
their nipples scarlet in a braver night.

Egypt Summer

An Appetizer of Radish & Cucumber

Marcela Sulak

Ingredients

Radishes
Young cucumbers
1 part sesame oil
2 parts rice vinegar
1 part tamari sauce
A good squeeze of lemon
Coarse ground black pepper to taste

Instructions

Take equal amounts of radish and young cucumber, wash and slice thinly.

Combine wet ingredients and shake until well mixed. Pour over the radishes and cucumbers and top with black pepper. I am more of a taste-as-you-go cook than a measurer. But no matter what the proportions, it always works.

Refrigerate until chilled, and serve.

Waldorf Salad

Amy Berkowitz

On a rainy night in October, dinner at Tasha's house is burgers and Waldorf salad, strange creamy dressing on apples and celery, the walnuts fall off our forks and we're laughing. There's beer and there's diet Snapple, and Tasha's mom is giddy off half a glass of ale, a smiling pink face in a fleece vest, and she's talking about a PBS special she saw, about what will happen when the magnetic fields reverse, and she's going off about it, she says the poles will shift, and we won't have just south and north anymore, we'll have poles all over the place, pulling us in every direction, and Tasha's dad asks twice what will happen to the planes and the migrating birds, but nobody answers, we're too busy inventing our own half-crazy questions and shouting them louder: Is it imminent? Will it happen suddenly, or will it be a gradual shift? Has it started already? What the fuck is a weather scientist? And Tasha's dad tries again, What will happen, and now he's laughing, What will happen to the planes and the birds? Our questions are hysterical and our eyes are on Tasha's mom. Okay, okay, she giddily continues, and then, since there are going to be poles everywhere, we'll be able to see the aurora borealis all the time, it will be beautiful, and—the room falls silent—and then everyone will get cancer! And we all burst out laughing, laughing so hard, laying down forks and grabbing the table for support, our hands over our mouths, our bodies shaking hard, hands slapping on the table, laughing and looking at each other laughing and laughing more. As the laughter subsides, we pick up our forks and start on our salads again. The cold crisp apples taste good, and death is a distant thing.

Waldorf Salad

Amy Berkowitz

Ingredients

2 large apples, cored and chopped (no need to peel)

½ cup chopped walnuts

½ cup red grapes, cut in half

2 tablespoons mayonnaise

2 tablespoons plain low-fat Greek yogurt

1 tablespoon lemon juice

Pinch of sea salt

1 cup chopped celery

Instructions

Whisk together mayonnaise, yogurt, lemon juice, and salt. Stir in the remaining ingredients, and chill until ready to serve.

Molecularity

Laura McCullough

We're in trouble;

a hungry accident is about to happen,

    and what science there is might turn

    out to be what saves us from us,

    a hot bowl held in both hands

    the only way to mark time.

Conditionality is unconditional:

    brains plastic after all,
humans one example of plastic art,

    all tape and welding, sponge

        and junk, glass and dried worms.
We sidle up to each other

    all bristle and solace—each the center of

        our own installation—our

    bones mellowing from red to yellow,

        and wanting to crack

            each other open. Is this all?   Bones

      like planets,

      like the sea,

drawn by music and gravity,

       the hum of those cells being born

       or dying, brains seemingly set

       inside themselves, but really just waiting

       for some new event, catastrophe,

             a singularity weighty as a thick, fatty stew?

Babies have more red marrow   adults more yellow,

       though in instances of severe blood loss, yellow

       is elastic, reforming into red,

similar to scavengers cracking open carcasses,

       predators left behind, scooping marrow. Cheap

       protein, fulsome,

       but a way to go on.

Vegetarian Stuffed Artichokes

Laura McCullough

Ingredients

Four large artichokes, the kind with the pointy spines on the leaves.
Bread crumbs
Oregano
Basil
Olive oil
Lemon
Grated parmesan cheese
Melted butter

Instructions

To prepare the artichokes, cut the leaves crosswise, and create flat surface.

Spread leaves open to get to center. Using peeler or grapefruit scooping spoon, get into the center, and remove the choke. Open the heads wide, and lay face down in a container of cold water with some lemon in it.

To prepare the stuffing, mix bread crumbs, oregano, basil, olive oil, lemon, grated parmesan cheese, and some melted butter. Stuff artichokes' centers, and spreading leaves, fill in between. Arrange in a pan with inch of water in bottom, and bake for an hour at 400° Fahrenheit.

Give each person a bowl with an artichoke with a lemon wedge next to it. Include a seafood fork, so diner can move some stuffing onto each leaf as they pull it off.

In center of table, place a large pretty platter or bowl.

Eat by peeling one leaf at a time, and draw across teeth to get stuffing and the meat of the leaf off. Toss the teeth marked leaves onto communal platter.

By end of meal, the platter is a ravaged mess.

Wine as needed.

Peaches

Barbara Crooker

In pecks and bushels
at Shoemaker's stand, they fill
the baskets with their golden heft,
their plush shoulders, handfuls
of light. Cut in wedges arranged
on a blue-glazed plate:
slices of sun in the August sky.
Take and eat, for this is the essence
of summer, given for you, in spite of
winter's sure return, the short grey days,
the icy nights. Right now, there are wheat
fields and sweet corn, daylilies and chicory
by the dusty roadsides; in the long dusk,
fireflies decorate the grass, rise up
to meet their doubles, the stars.

Tonight, there's fried chicken and sliced
tomatoes, hot biscuits, butter,
and peach jam. And later, you,
next to me on the rumpled
sheets, fuzz on the curve
of your cheeks and thighs,
your slick sweat on my skin.

And tomorrow, another hot one,
and that sweet juicy sun
will pop up again, staining
the horizon red, orange, gold.

Peach Marmalade

An Accompaniment to a Main Dish

Barbara Crooker

Ingredients

12 medium peaches, washed, peeled, pitted
3 medium oranges, washed, peel removed from half
Sugar (equal amount to fruit, around 6 cups)

Instructions

Spray a large kettle with PAM. Grind peaches and oranges in a blender. Measure; equal the amount of fruit with sugar.

Boil 25 minutes. Pour into jars, place on seals and lids, put in water bath canner.

Process 10 minutes.

Note: Red Haven peaches are the best. Look for seedless oranges.

How to Entertain

Anne Posten

Is this edible?
asked the Frenchwoman candidly,
bending to her host's ear with a Gallic
stage whisper.
The vulgar mosaic of meat,
fruit, sauce, sodden starches and
browbeaten greens broke
every culinary law she knew.
And where, at last, was the bread?
She laid down her knife:
From now on I shall cook.

From then on there was bread,
the food was pure
and well-salted.
The house pulsed with gourmet
elegance. His wife threw parties,
while the Frenchwoman plied her knife
with surety. He became accustomed.
The mosaics sparkled.

The meat fork lay between fish fork

and plate.

Is this livable?

he could not ask, thirty years later.

Alone, there was still bread.

Through the breakfast-room window,

untended flowers traced a fading mosaic.

He felt an impostor as he laid the table,

cheese, coffee, juice, meat.

A knife in each jar of glistening jam.

For years an understudy

to a role he had never hoped to play,

a perfect gentleman, sweeping no one

off her feet.

Anglo-French Cassis-Spiked Cranberry Sauce

Anne Posten

Ingredients

1 cup water
½ cup sugar
¼ cup plus 2 tablespoons crème de cassis (blackcurrant liqueur)
1 12 ounce bag fresh cranberries
1 cup dried cranberries
1 tablespoon ketchup

Instructions

Bring water, sugar, and ¼ cup crème de cassis to a boil in a medium saucepan over high heat, stirring to dissolve the sugar. Add fresh cranberries and return to the boil. Cook until berries pop and the sauce has thickened slightly, about 15 minutes. Remove from the heat and add dried cranberries, remaining crème de cassis, and ketchup. Chill for at least 4 hours and serve with turkey or roasted meat.

Serves 6

Other Women's Men

Claire McQuerry

Not that I am the type to move in.
Still, I can see why some women do,
brightening like the corner house that leaves
all their lights on: everyone knows

their kitchen walls are blue.
A flash of teeth or eyes that says
pay attention. All of us must hide
such hunger somewhere. Or,
if we are certain he loves her, the thrill

that he finds us interesting,
not for what we might offer in the end:
his question about my childhood trip to Russia
genuine, that hand he lifts to his glasses,
rubs around his neck, not affect but pure gesture.

I would like to believe this, as I crush the lime
over my glass, not trying to sparkle but not
not.
          This story about the car
he rebuilt in high school—

but people are all affect, I think
and then wait for sense

to catch up with his sound
so I can deliver the awaited response
with some extra show to compensate.

The way the young men at church,
newly married, avoid me or make
great show of wedding bands, why, at a potluck,
one whose wife is gone to her sister's in Tucson,
when I sit beside him, becomes deeply

fascinated by his pecan pie.
Some puritanical sensibility that sees an impure thought
far down the road and crosses to the opposite sidewalk—
even if that thought in the end is nothing
but a trick of sunlight.

There was a time, if we believe the stories,
when men and women didn't know their nakedness.

The afternoon in that shared kitchen
when I asked Sarah's husband about Amarene:
cherries soaked in syrup and brandy from the Friday market

and he crossed the room, holding the little clay jar,
unlidded it and lifted one cherry on a spoon,
the red syrup pooling the spoon's bowl,
and I opened my mouth to take
the bright fruit, closed my lips over the spoon,

only a moment, until a rat moved against a drain pipe
or I lifted a finger to wipe the syrup from my lip,
and we both saw how

close we stood, and he
turned quickly, setting

the jar aside, to scour at
the coffee staining
the sink.

Brandied Cherries

Claire McQuerry

Ingredients

1 ½ pounds sweet cherries (Washington Rainiers are wonderful,
   but any sweet cherry will do.)
¾ cup sugar
¾ cup water
2 tablespoons lemon juice
4 cardamom pods
1 cinnamon stick
1 cup brandy
1-quart jar with lid

Instructions

Rinse the cherries and remove stems. Boil the sugar, water, lemon juice, and spices in a medium saucepan for about 10 minutes, until liquid thickens. Remove saucepan from heat, stir in brandy, and add the cherries.

Allow the ingredients to cool completely (about one hour). Transfer cherries back to the jar and pour liquid over top. Seal jar and store in refrigerator. Wait at least one month before using the cherries. Delicious in cocktails or over ice cream for dessert.

Makes 2 quarts.

Cocktails

"Wine is bottled poetry."
—Robert Louis Stevenson

Amuse-Bouche

Claire Van Winkle

nf a morsel served before the hors d'oeuvre
lit. "to please the mouth"

for the Little Sparrow

—cleared my palate with her numb mouth

of morphine and champagne—

before the painted ladies,

a feast of faces in carnival colors.

A taste

in the setting of a starch-shouldered table,

its shroud, its crop circles of wheat-white wine—

the wounds where cups ran full and kept running.

The burgundy aged in her French oak mouth.

Her robin lips with their raven laugh—

her sex I'd mistake

for a dove.

But that first kiss—

rare, anesthetic,

a toast—

To the strong man, the piano,

to the clown,

Brava!

To the god of raised glasses and voices

raised in song.

Feast: Poetry & Recipes for a Full Seating at Dinner

La Violette

An Aperitif

Claire Van Winkle

Ingredients
per drink
one bottle of champagne allows for 4–6 drinks

20 milliliters of Violet Liqueur*
10 milliliters of St. Germain Elderflower Liqueur
Ice, for mixing
Champagne (or any dry sparkling wine)

Instructions
    1) Combine liqueurs and ice in a mixing glass.
    2) Strain liqueur into a chilled champagne flute.
    3) Fill the flute to the top with champagne.
    This drink can be enjoyed alone as an aperitif or as an accompaniment to an amuse-bouche. Pairs well with light delicacies such as oyster or caviar.

*Note: for the best results use a true violet liqueur, such as the Bitter Truth. However, sugar-based violet syrups (such as Monin Crème de Violette) are easy to find and can be used in this recipe for a sweeter cocktail or if violet liqueur is unavailable.

Georgina S. Francisco Is a Friend of Mine

Daniel A. Olivas

Georgina S. Francisco is a friend of mine,
and she is very particular about
two things: cheese and Margaritas.

"Cheese," she purrs, "must be strong,
sharp and sweet, like *dulce*."

She leans into me for emphasis.
"¿No?" she says through a red
O of a mouth.

"And there is only one way," she whispers,
"to make a Margarita."

I wave her off, my eyes bulging with
excitement, and tell her about my
latest Google search where I unearthed
the most remarkable Margarita recipe that
includes a bottle of beer.

Georgina's eyes narrow into mere slits,
and she spits out a disgusted, "Feh!"

Before I can say more, she stands and
looks down at me with disdain.
"There's only one way to make a Margarita,"
she sneers. "And it does *not* include beer."

Georgina turns on her heel leaving me
desolate with nothing more than her
perfume's scent and her rebuke's sting.

Georgina S. Francisco is a friend of mine,
and she is very particular about
two things: cheese and Margaritas.

Georgina's Margarita

Daniel A. Olivas

Ingredients

4 ounces Cointreau orange liqueur
4 ounces Grand Marnier orange liqueur
20 ounces sweet and sour mix
8 ounces lime juice
12 ounces tequila

Instructions

Mix ingredients in large mixing container. Fill eight salt rimmed glasses with ice. Add lime wedge or wheel to each glass. Pour mix into each glass.

Serves 8

Drinking Homebrewed Beer in Eddy's Kitchen

Lynn Hoffman

It's a brown-ale, light-weight, herbal, kinda sweet
It goes down quick like sea-foam bubbles popping on the beach.
Eddy's talking, telling the pictures on the wall—
The ones too rough for the parlor, too sweet for the shoe box:
Him in his Navy whites. Him on the Basketball court
with two boys, one dead, one moved to Arry-Zona.
His voice all light and white-thin as the peel of a garlic
just as dry, as likely to be blown away by a belch
or a puff of air.
Spinning spider threads-soft, sticky, weak and strong.
"The secret is honey," he says.
"That and some rosemary from the bush in the back."
He's talking about the beer, of course,
About what you bring from far away, what you keep at home.
There's a shot of their old house in Fishtown,
One of his Dad on a day when he was sober almost 'til dusk.
Another of Eddy and Kate in front of a cabin,
two little boys in mid-squirm on the steps.
Eddy rinses out the bottles, gets two more.
I ask about the black and white dog in the frame with the hearts.
"That's Buster," he says and then he can't say no more.
"Ah, don't get him started on his dear old dog," Kate says
"He's really just weepy for his lost childhood,"

she goes on like she was a TV show.
But I know Eddy's childhood, no honey, not much rosemary,
love mashed into nothin', ferment dried and gone.
"To Buster!" I say.
And Eddy and me, we drink to that.

Joan Ale June '08 White Tape

Lynn Hoffman

Ingredients

1 ½ cup rolled oats, mashed at 160° Fahrenheit

1 can wheat malt syrup 3.3 pounds

1 can light malt 3.3 pounds

1 cup caramel syrup

2 pounds honey

1 tablespoon ground juniper berries

1 cup brown sugar

Smidge of Malabar black pepper

Note: You can find these ingredients at a Homebrew Supply Store.

Instructions

Boil all ingredients for one hour.

Then add 1 ounce Sterling hops at 0 minutes

Followed by ½ ounce Strisselspat hops at 45 minutes.

Finally, add 1 ounce Strisselspat at 60 minutes.

Delicious, very food friendly. Next batch, brew with 4 pounds pilsner malt and Ardennes yeast in a smack pack.

Note: This recipe is geared toward a more experienced homebrewer. If you are new to homebrewing check out my The Short Course in Beer and shortcourseinbeer.blogspot. com, for more information.

My Wedding Toast

Diane Kendig

Here's to those who loved me not at daisy's end,
who could not love deep enough, love's labors
lost too soon, who never requited me
any time, any way.

To the too proud, too crazy, too sane, shy,
and rich, who found me immodest, unwealthy,
too noisy or quiet.

To the two-liter plastics—
all unreturnable—who did not turn over
my love, books, or heirlooms.

Here's to who screwed me, left me
unraveling, cleared out my lachrymals,
and to those much more passive
who left me intransitive.

My toast to them all, but the most toast to Paul,
my linguist, my lover,
my most very transitive.

Dawn's Wedding Punch

Diane Kendig

Ingredients
2 quarts champagne
2 quarts ginger ale
2 quarts white Sauternes wine
½ gallon orange or lemon sherbet

Instructions
Combine the first three ingredients, all well-chilled, while you melt the sherbet in the microwave. (Use defrost, then the lowest setting.) When the sherbet is melted, but not warm, stir it into the punch.

Notes:
1. This is a 1960's recipe, but still a great one. However, French Sauternes is not readily available. You can substitute any dessert wine, including a Riesling.
2. While the original recipe calls for orange or lemon sherbet, others can be used to match colors chosen for the party. We used raspberry for our parents' 50th anniversary fete.

Before Making a Toast

Marjorie Thomsen

You're mesmerized by the list of liquid destinations,
wondering where to get off tonight—
Italy for red or white, Brazil for orange liqueur
or Mexico, lured by a cilantro-tequila tincture.
Julia Child despised cilantro, threw it on the floor,
but you will hold your shapely condiments in admiration
after choosing a classic or new libation,
taking into consideration what spices up civilization—
cinnamon, clove and nutmeg swirling in a Sparkling Sangria
topped with bubbles popping heavenward, hypnotizing
your eyes, eyes that trust the beauty of surprise.
As with those you love, you can't wait to savor the soul,
the center of the hand-stuffed blue cheese olive bobbing
in a Martini, but then muddled, fresh-mint Mojito loiters lovely
and that's summer, a celebration of being
crushed under the weight of sunshine.
You arrive at antonym for August—Dark & Stormy—
charming bartender has obliterated the cliché of it,
behooved to use a boisterous ginger beer elixir,
triggering memories of those who rejoiced
before your time and you fancy the Southern Comfort
of Tennessee Williams (Stellaaaaaaa Artois?) to wassail with
as you summon his spirit to decide which decadence
should splash and spill, fill your crystal. Cocktails raised:
now it's time to offer the occasion, its players, their rightful accolades.

Sparkling Sangria

Marjorie Thomsen

Ingredients

5 liters of red Burgundy

8 ounces St. Germain

8 ounces Cherry Heering

8 ounces triple sec

8 ounces brandy

60 ounces orange juice

60 ounces cranberry juice

4 ounces simple syrup

Juice from 1 lemon

Juice from 1 lime

Juice from 1 whole grapefruit

12 ounces ginger beer

Instructions

Stir well, and serve on the rocks with 2 ounces sparkling rose, and a splash of ginger soda. Garnish with chopped pears and of course, if you'd like, add a dash of cinnamon, clove and nutmeg.

This makes a large batch. Scale down (or up) accordingly.

Note: A toast to charming bartender, Dave Werthman and West Side Lounge, Cambridge, Massachusetts, for this recipe.

The Usual

An Afternoon June Hailstorm in Jackson, Wyoming

Leah Shlachter

black sky
  pour

inside a tumbler
  5 count rain
  0 count lightningthunder
  6 count hail
ice   momentum
  muddle   crabapple
    blossom twists
  re lease: lilac flavors
and s h a k e
      cot
        —ton
         wood
    buds blend a
  splash of aspen   scents
    open sage
  chill   lupine wind

O sweet bartender!

strain sunlight
through cloud break

sip cocktail petals
      melt rocks to gutter
intoxicated pedestrians

Sage Gin Fizz

Leah Shlachter

(With thanks to Paul Wireman for the original recipe)

For each cocktail:

Muddle:
>—2 sage leaves
>—ice (enough to fill 1 glass)

Add:
>—6 count Hendrick's Gin
>—2 count simple syrup
>—2 count lemon juice

Shake or Stir

Top off with:
>—soda

Garnish:
>—lemon wedge
>—sage leaf

Sangria & Ceviche, Santiago's Bodega, Key West, Florida

Joe Wilkins

> *One hypothesis suggests that the common Spanish word for the dish,*
> cebiche, *has its origin in the Latin word* cibus, *which translates to*
> *English as "food for men and animals."*
> —Wikipedia

Of an evening we come wineful & glad,

each streetlight a shawl for your bare shoulders,

that gravel alley possible & tempting

as my hunger. In a house whisper-dark

& clattery, & among our hungry,

sun-dazed kind, we sit & against the heat

sip wine over ice. Between us now some god

sees fit to set a blue earthen bowl

brimming with the sunrise flesh of yellowfin,

with flowers drooped unto fruit, mango

& alligator pear, with onion's red root

& cilantro's bright leaf, with a fiery slick

of lime & habanero, sea salt's gritty, necessary

kiss. Lover, we are right to pray

no grace. Lover, we are wrong. This supper,

like all love & supper, is animal & sacred.

We ought to eat raw & wild & know

beneath every saintly skin the fever blood

yet races. We ought to fast to idiocy

& chant praiseful litanies, know the world is world

& more. Oh, this night let our only penance

be to heft the bowl & despite the stares

lick the blue stone clean, then down Pentecost sing

our happy way home, there give ourselves

to other hungers. Oh, later, let it be later—

if that other penance might wait a year, a day—

please, an hour—yet even as we lip

the final runnel of salt & fire, like hunger

I feel it rising, remaking this & every hunger,

memory's empty succor & sweet sting.

White Sangria

Joe Wilkins

Ingredients

2 apples
2 pears
2 oranges
1 cup white rum
½ cup triple sec
2 bottles dry white wine
Lime slices

Instructions

Core and dice apples and pears. Peel and dice oranges. Combine fruit in a large bowl. Pour the rum and triple sec over the fruit and cover the bowl. Chill in the refrigerator for a few hours.

In a pitcher, mix the chilled fruit and liquor with chilled white wine. Serve over ice in deep wine glasses and garnish each glass with a lime slice.

Note that all sorts of additions and substitutions can be made here according to taste, just as long as you've got some fruit, liquor, and wine in the mix. Also note that the ceviche simply can't be recreated. Get yourself to Santiago's Bodega in Key West if you want some.

Abraham Lincoln Raises a Glass to Robert Burns in the Afterlife

Kathleen Kirk

Once, asked to raise a toast to you,
I was struck dumb.

But here we all are, rattling and dust.
The sounds we make
might not frighten a mouse.

What hurts most, I know you know it,
is the harm we ourselves have done,
not what was done to us.

I do not mean to mumble, or go silent again.
Not here, in the lilac fog.

Here, all I can remember is joy—
dancing with a fine woman, the heart of the wood
when I split it, my mother when I was a child.

You and Shakespeare!
And Mr. Whitman.
Ah, Willie! Ah, Tad, ah—!

All my boys, all my boys!

Lilacs in the Courtyard Cosmo

Kathleen Kirk

Ingredients

1 ½ ounce vodka

1 ounce Cointreau or triple sec

½ ounce fresh lime juice

¼ ounce cranberry juice

Dash of blueberry liqueur (you want a lilac sweetness) or
   Blue Curaçao (which has a citrus tang) for lilac color

Instructions

   Shake ingredients with ice in cocktail shaker or Boston shaker and strain into chilled conical cocktail (martini) glass. Garnish with spiral of orange or lime peel or wedge of lime & sprig of lilac. Sprig of lilac can be used as boutonnière if preferred! Most impressive when mixed individually in the presence of the one about to drink it! Have all ingredients, and garnish, at hand. Repeat above steps for each drink.

Serves 1

In Vino Veritas

Diane Kendig

This is about truth in wine. My first glass was a thick tumbler
of Mogan David in Westerville in 1970, though I usually lie
and say a pitcher of sangria in Spain in '71 that made
the Gothic cathedral revolve on the Plaza Mayor.
For me, only these years were outstanding for wine,
the ones since, stupendous, so I'm deaf as you discuss vintages,
soil, weather, luck, and you flinch when I talk about the jugs and jugs
of *corriente* carried up and around mountains,
what was cheap, local, ubiquitous.
We each glower over our glass container, yours with labels,
numbers, names, and dates, as though there is wine in your truth.
But no, love, I'm seeking the truth in the wine, and for that,
any bottle will do.

Dandelion Blossom Wine

Diane Kendig

Ingredients

1 gallon washed dandelion blossoms
3 pounds sugar
Juice from two lemons
Handful of raisins

Instructions

Pour 1 gallon boiling water over the 1 gallon washed dandelion blossoms. Let stand for 24 hours. Strain. Place the strained liquid in a crock and to it, add sugar, the lemon and raisins. Cover and let this all stand for four to five days, skimming off the froth that rises to the top occasionally. After the four to five days, strain the liquid again, pour it into bottles and cap them till the liquid stops working. (This will take several weeks.) At the end of this period, cap the bottles tightly, and let the wine ripen for at least four months.

Note: This is the only wine I have ever made, under the influence of Ray Bradbury's Dandelion Wine, which I was reading with the students at my first teaching job, a tiny school in the middle of a farming community. One spring day after school, a group of them came to my room with a trash bags, and one said, "Come on, Miss Kendig, my mom says we need to pick the dandelions now for you to make that wine." And about five of us set out into the field to pick. I found several recipes, pieced them together into this one, and set about making and waiting. It turned out wonderful and beautiful, a gorgeous golden color.

The History of Watermelon

Marcela Sulak

Imagine a desert, with real sand, with cracked stones
the color of furnaces, ash-rimmed and glowing
with heat—not an analogy for your own
barrenness—this is a desert. The black granite groans
in the fissures of daybreak, your dry thirsty tongue
stumbles upon a band of nomadic syllables. Here are
the dust-covered hoof prints of livestock, the lizards
that thrive in the shadows, the wind driving forward, the sun.
It is tomorrow or last year or eight thousand years
ago. Time doesn't matter, before you, a tawny
vine languidly stretches as if it were yawning,
the wind parts her leaves, then one hundred melons appear
warm to the touch. Broken open, the pale wet mouths spill
their sweet water, crisp water—now drink your fill.

Watermelon Margaritas

Marcela Sulak

Ingredients

4 ½ cups watermelon, chilled, seeded and cut into pieces

¾ cups lime juice, freshly squeezed

¾ cups silver (white) tequila

¾ cups Triple Sec (or Cointreau)

24 large ice cubes

Instructions

Blend the watermelon, mix in the rest; coat the rim of your margarita glass with coarse salt and garnish with a lime.

Serves 6

Feast: Poetry & Recipes for a Full Seating at Dinner

Paradise on the Head of a Pin

Laura McCullough

In the room where he waits, hunger
has become his friend and confidante.
When hunger returned after a long trip,
he ran toward it like a lost lover back
from desert travails with exotic stories
of horses and wild fruit. Now, he holds
hunger in his arms murmuring, tell me,
again, those stories. The details never
change, and, as time goes on, he begins
to tell the stories himself, so by heart
he knows them. After some time, they
have nothing left to tell. There is no
gnawing in his gut, though hunger
is there. In the pale light, clearly the bet
has been lost; he is satiated by hunger.
In all fairness, shouldn't god let him go?

Tell Stories & Sip

Laura McCullough

Water. Flat as well as sparkling.
Glasses found while thrift store scavenging.
Offer guests a choice of glass.
Offer guests choice of water.
Sip slowly.
Tell each other stories.

Alternately, offer vodka instead of water.

Tell each other stories.

I Serve It Forth

Sarah Yasin

Come. Sit on my lap.
I shall feed you whole
pleasures from my hand:
blueberry waffles with
smooth clotted cream,
strong Irish coffee,
currants and cherries,
pastry with mascarpone.
I shall place fine delectation
into your mouth and you
will stretch up for more.

Irish Coffee

Sarah Yasin

Ingredients

5 cups brewed hot coffee
1 pint whiskey (or 2 fingers per drink)
10 teaspoons brown sugar (one per drink)
1 pint heavy cream

Instructions

Warm the mugs in any fashion. Individually, mix the coffee, whiskey, and sugar in glass mugs. Then slowly pour a jigger of cream over the back of a spoon into a prepared mug so that it floats on the surface of the coffee. Repeat for all the mugs. Do not mix the two layers together. Do not whip the cream: the cream is a layer through which the coffee is drunk. So smooth, so agreeable.

Serves 10

Mains

"He hath eaten me out of house and home."
—Shakespeare, *Henry the Fourth*

Ingredients

Martha Silano

In one ear the crunch of *kapusta*—in the other the sizzle
of *bacala*. Through one nostril the deep, dark sting

of hot olive oil meeting garlic—through the other the steam
of cheddar cheese suffusing mashed potato peaks.

Some nights our burps told tales of *halushki*—
egg and flour plopped into swirling water,

then fried with buttery cabbage unfurling
past Poland, past Austria-Hungary, all the way back

to Mother Russia. Some nights the basil in *pasta siciliana*
sweetened our breath till dawn—our *sogni dori* green fields

skirting the Adriatic. Surely some of what they cooked
commingled—garlic-laden kielbasa, *galumpkis* swimming

in a thick tomato sauce—but mostly what they sautéed or steamed
married only completely in their children,

the four of us who entered their kitchen—little rumbling Etnas,
hollow perogies longing to be filled—who raised our glasses—*Salute!*—

to the bulka and to provolone, to all things *schmatzhnee* and *dolce*,
who left each night, a few flecks of pepper, a sprig of parsley,

still clinging to our teeth.

Grandmom Victoria's Halushki

(Fried Cabbage with Dumplings)

Martha Silano

Ingredients:

For the fried cabbage:

1 large head cabbage

1 medium-sized onion

2 cloves garlic

4 tablespoons unsalted butter

2 tablespoons vegetable oil

1 teaspoon sugar (brown or white is fine)

Salt and black pepper

For the egg-flour dumplings:

2 cups white flour

2 eggs

½ teaspoon salt

Scant amount water (optional, depending on consistency of the dough)

Instructions

For the fried cabbage:

    Chop cabbage in thin strips or shred it if you prefer.

    Chop the onions.

    Smash and finely chop the garlic cloves.

    Melt the butter in a large iron skillet set to medium heat.

    Add the vegetable oil.

Add the onions and garlic. Sauté for 3 minutes.

Add the cabbage and cook until limp.

Toss in the sugar. Add salt and pepper to taste.

For the egg-flour dumplings:

Begin boiling a saucepan of lightly salted water.

Measure two cups of white flour into a medium-sized bowl.

Break in first egg, mixing with a fork until blended.

Add in the second egg, blending thoroughly.

The mixture should be gloppy and sticky.

Dollop heaping-sized teaspoonfuls of dough into pot of boiling water.

Retrieve dumplings with a slotted spoon as soon as they begin to float to the top.

Pour dumplings atop the cabbage mixture and stir. Adjust seasonings. Serve immediately.

Serves 6–10

When Cabbage Is Not a Vegetable

Michele Battiste

Your mother would make it
better. You mother would
shake her head at such skinny
noodles. *Who can taste*
such a skinny noodle your mother
would ask. Your mother would
serve it with hard-crusted peasant
bread. When you lecture your mother
about double carbs, your mother
looks at you like you are
a disappointment. When you ask
your mother about the vegetables,
she looks at you like you are
something too precious and already
broken. *What? Cabbage isn't*
a vegetable, your mother asks. *Have*
a pickle, then. Here, have a pickle.
A pickle your mother made with bread
and dill and a rusty cap and you
have never been able to make
these pickles. No one you know
who attempted these pickles
has ever succeeded. They are
the pickles her mother made and when
you serve your mother *káposztás tészta*,

the cabbage too thick, the noodles
unsubstantial, your mother will shrug
and nod and eat and you will smile
at your mother and your mother
will remind you about the pickles and you
will remind your mother about the time
she put diet coke in your son's
baby bottle and your mother
will sigh and say that one day, too,
you will be a grandmother and you
will make the *káposztás tészta*
and you will make the pickles and you
will make the memories with your
grandchild and your child will say
no one can make these pickles like
my mother makes these pickles, these
are the pickles that her mother made.

Káposztás Tészta
(Cabbage Noodle)

Michele Battiste

Ingredients

One large head of cabbage
1 pound of egg noodles (I like medium, my mother likes wide)
1 cup of salt
Black pepper to taste (and by taste, I mean a ton)
½ cup of olive oil

Instructions

Shred or chop the cabbage. (My mother uses a cheese grater and shreds it very fine. I use the slicer on my food processor, which for some reason mildly exasperates my mother, and it turns out thicker. I have, in the past, also just chopped it up with a knife.) In a big bowl, coat cabbage evenly and pretty thickly with salt. At first, it should feel a bit grainy. Let it sit for one to three hours before cooking, turning it over occasionally. (The finer it's shredded, the less time the salt marinade will take.) It should be extremely wilted.

Rinse.

When you're ready to begin cooking take a handful of the rinsed, wilted cabbage and squeeze the bejeezus out of it. And all of the excess water. You have to squeeze really hard. (This is my least favorite step because my hands get tired. If you have a friend around, make him help.) After squeezing, put the cabbage in a large frying pan. Repeat this step until all the cabbage has had the bejeezus and the water squeezed out of it and is in the frying pan.

Fry the cabbage in most of the oil on medium heat. Stir occasionally. Add more oil if the cabbage sticks or seems to need it. You be the judge. Season with lots of black pepper. More than you would think.

While the cabbage is frying, boil your noodles to the desired state of doneness.

The cabbage is done frying when it has turned a lovely caramel-y shade of brown and smells really good. Mix the cabbage into the noodles to a ratio that you find pleasing. I like A LOT of cabbage in my noodles. You can freeze or refrigerate any leftover fried cabbage to mix with fresh egg noodles another time.

Serve with a green salad, a bean soup, crusty bread, Hungarian *pálinka*.

Cabbage, a Love Song

Marcela Sulak

I dislike you, cabbage. Your tight-fisted order
yielding to my little knives with your
immaculate squeaks. Your rotund indifference to all
that falls away. The fact you feed me through the winter,
through the centuries, and I dislike my need,
the shadows of my lifting fingers cast by your
green light, and all my old sorrow. I dislike
your density, as if the world lacked space, your pure
white heart that open fields can't heat, the way
you fall apart when cooked. You're such a poor loser.
Plus it takes so very long to finish all of you.
I can say without reservation, I hate
all the casual ways you're so unseemly chaste,
so haughty in your modesty, so moderately good.

Cabbage Fritters

Marcela Sulak

Ingredients

½ small head of cabbage
Small, finely cut zucchini
1 shredded carrot
4–6 tablespoons sesame seeds
1 teaspoon sesame oil
1–2 tablespoons minced ginger root
1–2 cloves garlic, finely chopped
2 eggs
Pinch salt
4 tablespoons flour

Instructions

Combine all and fry in light, hot oil, like a pancake.

Note: The quantities are approximate, as I don't really measure anything. Cabbage is very forgiving.

The Wet, Then Dry Ingredients, xi

Robby Nadler

        i sat memorizing names of unknown seasonings
you twisted my gaze from the chin
thought you were going to kiss me
but you didn't
you pressed your bogey man fingers into the canyons of my cheeks
stared into my eyes for something stashed beyond the pupil
examined me like the doctors had all week
your hands your stethoscope
your eyes your m.r.i.
and then finally you did kiss me
your lips your blood panel
cooking is a science you began
food is a series of chemical reactions of chemical states
if a soup is too spicy add cream
the casein will diffuse the fatty capsaicin like soap on grease
you grated chopped sliced baked sautéed stuffed chilled warmed
scooped breaded sprinkled served
your body as if it were a visible dictionary of verbs
all medicine
a pill is a soup that feeds a disease
a soup is a pill that cures the soul
each body resonates a mood a thought a desire
when you read a menu you aren't picking food

hidden in your deepest unevolved brain
a voice echoes
feed me this
a chef is a pharmacist with a spatula
i slipped off the head of the stool
what did my body tell you
the flour had still not settled
your symptoms are coldness and hunger
cold because you feel alone
hunger because there is so much in you yet to be done
this time i kissed you
and forty-five minutes later
we sat together at your table
acorn squash boats
stuffed a with yam and sweet potato puree
mixed with zante currants
roasted walnuts gruyere and blue cheese
brown sugar southwestern heat
dolloped over a berry maple syrup butter glaze
baked with ciabatta breadcrumbs and bacon bits
a boat of leek shitake gravy to douse the embedded serranos
in that moment i understood
the smell of the food trickling in
and i could taste the desire in your head
the empathy for each flavor to be known and loved by a discerning tongue
food as token of lasting want
the physical decaying but the urge to eat ever-thriving
long past our own demise in the people
who will remember us
and those who won't

Acorn Squash Stuffed with Spicy Sweet Potato Filling

Robby Nadler

Ingredients

1 medium sweet potato

2 acorn squashes

25 grams raisins

25 grams walnuts, chopped

50 grams Gruyere cheese, shredded

8 tablespoons of brown sugar

4 tablespoons butter

1 Serrano pepper, chopped

Bread crumbs

1 teaspoon nutmeg

1 teaspoon black pepper

1 teaspoon salt

1 teaspoon granulated garlic

½ teaspoon cinnamon

Instructions

Preheat an oven to 170° Celsius. Peel the sweet potato and poke holes in it with a fork. Bake the sweet potato for forty-five minutes until ready to puree in a blender, hand mixer, or food processor. (A hand masher will work fine, but you won't get the same smoothness). Let puree fully cool in the refrigerator (overnight works).

Wash the squash and cut in half along the horizontal axis. Scoop out the seeds with a spoon or ice cream scoop.

Combine the Serrano, raisins, cheese, walnuts, spices, 4 tablespoons of sugar, and salt with the puree. Add a tablespoon of butter and sugar to the natural cup in the squash half. Add a quarter of the puree over. Top with bread crumbs.

Bake at 170° Celsius for 1 hour or until the acorn squash is softened.

Serves 4–8

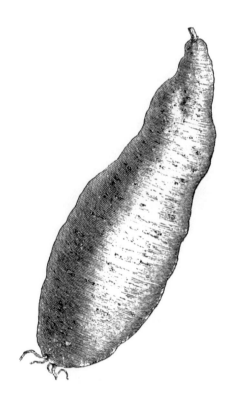

The History of Brussels Sprouts

Marcela Sulak

This vegetable evolved from primitive
non-heading Mediterranean kraut.
It wrapped its crinkly little leaves about
its winsome, blooming face and left to live
a classic *Bildungsroman*. Adjusting mien
and flavor, traveling north and west, it came
upon the gates of Brussels, took the name
that welcomed it. Gentlemen and lean
courtesans took into their mouths its tight
green jackets, endlessly disrobing, sheets
of luminosity pressed close. And fleets
dispatched to newer worlds carried wide
and far its seed. Like any immigrant,
it put down roots before it could repent.

Roasted Brussels Sprouts

Marcela Sulak

Ingredients

1 ½ pounds Brussels sprouts, ends trimmed and yellow leaves removed
3 tablespoons olive oil
1 teaspoon kosher salt
½ teaspoon freshly ground black pepper

Instructions

Preheat oven to 400° Fahrenheit (205° Celsius).

Place trimmed Brussels sprouts, olive oil, kosher salt, and pepper in a large resealable plastic bag. Seal tightly, and shake to coat. Pour onto a baking sheet, and place on center oven rack.

Roast in the preheated oven for 30 to 45 minutes, shaking pan every 5 to 7 minutes for even browning. Reduce heat when necessary to prevent burning. Brussels sprouts should be darkest brown, almost black, when done. Adjust seasoning with kosher salt, if necessary. Serve immediately.

There are more poetic ways to cook and serve brussels sprouts. You can steam them with baby potatoes and carrots, then toss them with fresh mint and basil, butter, salt and pepper, for example. But to be honest, they taste really good roasted. But whatever you do with them, serve them with a chilled white wine. That will help them disrobe on the tongue.

Patrimonial Recipe

Daniele Pantano

I swore never to wear my father's mask

Yet I meticulously peel and cut tomatoes.
Crush garlic. Pluck basil bent
Low in observance. One
By one. Push them off the plank.

Into the fervid blonde of olive oil.

Salt. Pepper. Dash of sugar.
Then I sit down at the table.
Yell at my children for being children.
Ignore my wife—her voice:

The steam of boiling water.

And wait for the perfect consistency.
Al dente. The callous core that weeps

When overcooked.

Sugo di Pomodoro

(Basic Tomato Sauce)

Daniele Pantano

Ingredients

4 pounds of ripe tomatoes
5 tablespoons of extra-virgin olive oil
6–8 cloves of garlic (slightly crushed)
1 small bunch of fresh basil leaves
2 teaspoons of sugar
1 teaspoon of crushed red pepper
Sea salt and freshly ground black pepper to taste

Instructions

Peel, seed, and chop the tomatoes. Heat the olive oil in a large skillet. Add garlic and sauté over a medium flame until garlic begins to turn golden. Add chopped tomatoes, salt, basil, crushed red pepper, black pepper, and sugar.

Reduce the flame to low and simmer, stirring frequently, until the sauce has thickened, about 15–20 minutes. Serve sauce over your favorite pasta, or with meatballs.

Company Is Coming

M.J. Iuppa

(I smooth the puckered linen,
wishing it were carefree, but

my table sets in old-fashioned
stubbornness. I'm still inclined

to woo and cluck over creases,
tying soft knots in each corner;

my hands tug for tenderness.
It gives a little.)

Blue candles. Warm bread,
A knock at the door.

Chop, Chop … Fresh Tomato Sauce over Bow Ties

M.J. Iuppa

Ingredients

5–6 tomatoes (medium to large size)
½ sweet onion (Vidalia)
5–6 fresh mushrooms (washed and patted dry)
8 baby carrots
1 small red or yellow or orange pepper
5–6 leaves of fresh basil (at least)
1–2 baby zucchini
1–2 small yellow squash
2–3 tablespoons olive oil
2 cloves of garlic (minced)
Salt (to taste)
Pepper (to taste)
Red pepper flakes (to taste)
1 box of bow tie pasta
2 tablespoons grated Romano cheese
2 tablespoons of butter

Instructions

Rough chop all ingredients from tomatoes to basil. Thin slice zucchini and yellow squash, then cut the discs in half.

Put all chopped and sliced ingredients in a ceramic 2 quart bowl, then add olive oil, minced garlic, salt, pepper and red pepper flakes.

Now gently stir all the ingredients and let sit in bowl. Cover bowl.

Prepare 1 box of bow ties according to package. Drain macaroni then put it back into kettle. Add butter to hot macaroni. Stir gently, coating the bow ties evenly. Add grated Romano cheese and toss gently again.

Put serving of bow ties on individual plates. Top with the fresh sauce and another sprinkle of Romano cheese.

You can serve this with grilled sausage, if you desire, a small fresh salad, and, of course, bread.

Don't forget to light the blue candles. This is a heavenly summer meal.

Anniversary Tajarin

Matthew Gavin Frank

She loves the stewing together
of horseshit, eucalyptus,
and rain. She can't get

a handle on ice skates with pink
laces, the road atlas of British
Columbia, mussels that refuse

to open, even in all of this
broth. Like cabbage in a pan,
we don't realize we're cabbage—

it is the egg that unites us...

Tajarin with Savoy Cabbage, Mushroom, Hazelnut and Sage Butter

Matthew Gavin Frank

Tajarin is like the Piemontese Italian version of tagliatelle, but cut a bit thinner. This recipe can work just as easily with fettuccine, linguine, and spaghetti cuts of pasta as well. This recipe calls for fresh pasta (which will really make the dish sing), but dried pasta can be substituted if time is an issue.

Ingredients

For the pasta dough:
1 ¾ cups all-purpose flour, unbleached and sifted
2 teaspoons olive oil
2 teaspoons milk
6 large egg yolks
1 large egg

For the sauce:
5 tablespoons unsalted butter
¼ cup finely chopped fresh sage leaves
2 sage leaves per plate for garnish
1 cup sliced mushrooms
1 cup chiffonade of Savoy cabbage
¼ cup chopped hazelnuts (can substitute walnuts, if necessary)

2 cloves garlic, finely chopped

½ cup onion, chopped or thinly sliced

1 tablespoon olive oil

1 teaspoon balsamic vinegar

Salt and pepper to taste

Parmigiano-Reggiano cheese for garnish, freshly grated or
    finely chopped

Instructions

For the pasta dough:

On a clean, dry work surface, heap the flour into a mound, then create a circular well in the center. Into the well, add the remaining wet ingredients. With your index finger slowly stir the wet ingredients in a circular motion, until the surrounding flour incorporates slowly. Once the dough begins to thicken a bit, fold the remaining flour into the well and knead the dough 15–20 minutes, until it is smooth, not sticky, and a bit elastic. (Initially, the dough will look a bit ragged). Wrap the dough ball in plastic wrap and let rest 30 minutes. Clean the work surface. With a knife, cut the dough ball into 4 equal sized pieces. Keep the remaining pieces plastic wrapped while working with each. Dust the work surface with a bit of flour and, with a rolling pin, roll each section of the dough ball until it is about ⅛ inch thick. If you have a hand-crank (or electric) pasta roller, this step is a breeze. With the roller, pass the dough through the widest setting three times. Switch to a thinner setting, and repeat. Continue until you have reached the thinnest setting. With a knife, carefully cut your pasta to desired "noodle" width. Some pasta rollers have a setting for this step as well. Dust the cut pasta with coarse cornmeal (to prevent sticking), and set in a loose pile, until you have finished this process with the remaining dough.

Cooking the fresh pasta:

In boiling, lightly salted water, boil until cooked (for fresh pasta, this should take about 2 minutes or so. The pasta can be made ahead and frozen. To work with the frozen pasta, DO NOT DEFROST IT. Simply add the frozen pasta to the boiling salted water and allow to cook until finished (only about 3 minutes or so). Drain in colander. In colander, drizzle small amount of olive oil over the pasta, and stir to prevent sticking.

For the sauce:

In a dry skillet, over medium heat, toast the chopped hazelnuts, circulating them throughout the pan to prevent burning, for about 2 minutes. Remove from pan and set aside. Add olive oil to pan and sauté the onion and cabbage, stirring occasionally, about 4 minutes. Add the mushrooms, garlic, and hazelnuts and cook, stirring constantly, for one minute. Add the balsamic vinegar, and cook, stirring occasionally for another 2 minutes. Add the butter and chopped sage, and lower the heat to medium-low. Cook, stirring occasionally, for about 1 minute. Season to taste with salt and pepper.

To finish:

Either portion the pasta onto plates and drizzle the sauce over the top, or add the pasta to the sauce skillet, and toss to coat. Garnish each plate first with Parmigiano-Reggiano cheese, then the 2 sage leaves, arranged in a V at the top center of the pasta. Eat noisily.

Serves 8

Eggs Satori

Karen Greenbaum-Maya

Take an egg for each eater,
another for the pan.
The eggshells should be opaque,
too bright to look at if white, freckled matte if brown.
Crack the eggs into a generous bowl.
Use your entire arm, wrist hand forearm shoulder as one.
Achieve a decisive snap that strikes the shell cleanly
        at the bowl's edge.
Empty each eggshell of its little world.

Heat the frying pan, only just enough
to melt a lump of butter the size of a nut, any nut.
Float the pan off the stove.
While the pan cools, whisk the eggs
        as mildly as wind ruffles grass.
No bubbles. No froth. A slosh of cream does no harm.
Pockets of egg white will bob to the surface.
Accept this. Add salt.

When you can pat the underside of the pan
as you would pat a friend's shoulder,
return the pan to a gentle heat.
Quietly, pour in the beaten eggs. Now, leave them.
Chop some fresh tarragon, or a small ripe tomato.
Bring this to your eggs.

Let them all get acquainted in their own time.
Drag a fork languidly through the eggs,
where a small buffer is starting to thicken.
Let your lungs fill and subside without effort. Release the breath.

Gently tour the rest of the pan.
Drag the fork around the edge again.
Now the eggs will start to yield large curds.
Observe this without urgency. Low heat. No bubbles.
Bring drifts of egg to the center,
slowly enough to feel their mute resistance
to the pull of the fork. So slight, the weight.
If curds break into pieces, you are working too hard.
You have been dragged off-center.
Stop. Get over yourself.
Let the eggs cook alone for a moment.
Honor how little they require from you.

Gather the eggs together at the center of the pan.
Coax them to turn over. Turn off the flame.
Gaze around the kitchen a moment,
take the pan from the burner.
Divide the billowy mass into portions and serve.
Eat your egg in small voluptuous bites. Do not speak.

Rice & Eggs

Sheila Squillante

Rainy Sunday and he let me
sleep in. When I woke, broken
after weeks of stress and uncertainty,
job angst, self-doubt, I needed

eggs—cracked in a porcelain bowl, olive
oil swirling in a hot pan
and the leftover curry from last night's
dinner: potatoes, lentils and brown

basmati, infused with ginger, cumin
seed and cloves. I needed to hear
the sizzle and sear,
feel the spatula press the mixture

thickly against the bottom. I needed to pour
the pale yellow over everything
and watch it seep between the rice
and lentils, glaze the potatoes.

This is the meal I prepared
and shared with him this morning.
I heaped mango chutney onto my plate
and he drizzled Sriracha onto his.

I forgot the cilantro but it didn't matter.
Spicy, sweet, unctuous and filling. Warm
and comforting. I remembered
that my grandmother used to

make rice & eggs for breakfast for my father
as a boy. Peasant food elevated to iconic
levels. And I know she made it for me, too,
but I cannot say that I remember exactly

what it tasted like. I think hers was more
eggs than rice, something of a porridge.
Maybe she used cheese? Seasonings,
surely—oregano, maybe? I don't know, but

it doesn't matter. I remember
the *feeling*—tender rice, soft eggs,
burnished with butter,
glistening in my mouth, in my gut;

the way it promised,
in my grandmother's voice,
"Everything will be fine. Here,
my baby, have another bite."

Rice & Eggs

Sheila Squillante

Ingredients

1 dozen fresh eggs
1 quart leftover take-out rice (I always order extra just
    so I can make this the next day)
Olive oil
Sesame oil
Salt & white pepper
Sriracha ("Rooster Sauce") or other hot chili paste to taste

Instructions

Scramble eggs in a large ceramic bowl. Cobalt blue looks very pretty against sunny yellow. Add a teaspoon salt and ½ teaspoon white pepper (or to taste).

Heat large non-stick skillet or well-seasoned stainless steel wok over medium heat for one minute. Add 1 tablespoon olive oil and a drop or two of sesame oil to the pan. Swirl and heat for one minute.

Working in batches, add cold rice to cover the bottom of the pan, breaking it up and pushing it down into one layer. Listen to it sizzle and resist the urge to stir it for a minute or two. It's nice to have it a little crispy. Turn it with a silicone spatula. Press it down again.

Pour some of the egg mixture over the rice, letting it seep in between the grains. (Add a little more oil if necessary.) Either scramble the whole mess or let it cook a bit before attempting to flip it like a pancake. It doesn't have to be pretty but it is going to be delicious. When eggs are cooked through, pop it into a warm oven while you repeat the process for the remaining rice & eggs.

Serve on a large platter or as individual portions. Give it another sprinkle of salt, a tiny drizzle of sesame oil, a larger drizzle of Sriracha.

If it happens to be summer and you happen to have cilantro taking over your garden, throw on a few leaves. Ripe mango, watermelon and kiwis would be nice on the side. As would a pot of strong coffee and a pitcher of Bloody Marys.

Serves 6

The Kitchen Weeps Onion

James Arthur

      The kitchen weeps onion
because the cook is dead. Pans strike chorus
and the ladles keep a knock-kneed stride.
      Burners gleam more brightly. Chives,
chives, and chives. Everyone seems so tired
but the diners can't sleep. The kitchen tonight
weeps onion, so everyone else must weep.
      What's the use in talking? Let's touch,
and turn apart. The cook is quiet,
      cold, unearthly, and the turnip
      breaks its heart.

Seahorse Fettuccine

James Arthur

I created this recipe while living in northwest Missouri and working as an instructor of freshman composition. One of my roommates was a cook, and that forced me to step up my game in the kitchen; as a broke student, I'd always thought of pasta as a necessary evil. Once I learned a little more about cooking, I came to appreciate that noodles could be vehicle for things other than cold Ragu.

This is one of the first dishes that I cooked for the woman who's now my wife, so I guess it turned out okay.

Ingredients

3 good-sized onions, diced
8 cloves of garlic, minced
3 tablespoon olive oil
3 28-ounce tins of diced tomatoes
1½ tablespoons thyme
1 ½ tablespoons basil
1 ½ tablespoons oregano
Several generous grinds of black pepper
⅓ cup horseradish
1 ½ pound cooked medium-sized shrimp
½ cup chopped chives
3 pounds fettuccini

Instructions

In a large saucepan over medium heat, cook onions and garlic with olive oil until onions are translucent. Add tomatoes, undrained, and bring to a boil. Once the tomatoes are boiling, add spices, then reduce heat, and simmer with lid on for 20 minutes or until the sauce has reduced by one third. Add horseradish and shrimp; simmer for 5 minutes with lid off. Add chives and simmer for 5 minutes more.

Serve over fettuccini.

Serves 6–10

The Song of Fontina

Erin Elizabeth Smith

> *The poets have been mysteriously*
> *silent on the subject of cheese.*
> —GK Chesterton

It is true. I have sung of April blackberries,
toothy shallots, young romas on the vine.
I have praised the thump-round crisp
of peppers and the bushy basil
in Mississippi.

I have troubadoured the wood ear
mushroom, lemon zest in the winey
risotto. Praised the practical meanness
of artichokes and shucked shimmer
of Gulf oysters.

And of wine and beer and the icy
caramel lick of good bourbon,
I have volumes. Such love
for the delicate hold of stems,
malbec tails in the glassware,
decanters, pint glasses, the perfect
ice crystals of well-shaken martinis.

But cheese—
the grocery store islands of cheese,
the art party tables of cheese,

the lickable glass of French fromageries.
The camemberts, parmesans, bries.

O I want to sing you cheese.
The smoked gouda
wonder of pasta. Goat cheese purpled
with merlot. Or imported feta,
that sheen of new cheese
from its brine.

Want to sing the blue cheese potatoes,
the fist-round mozzarella.
Sing the wholly Swiss triangle,
the muenster with portobello.

And all the times in the party-dark,
whiskey-blinded, when I grated pepperjack
into that drunk béchamel, while the poets
lumbered in from front porch cigarettes,
scooped the corn-blue chips into the rich,
white sauce. Silenced, for a second,
we sang and we sang
with our mouths closed.

Tequila-Marinated Shrimp and Jack Cheese Nachos

Erin Elizabeth Smith

Ingredients

For the shrimp:

1 pound medium shrimp, peeled & deveined

¼ cup tequila

¼ cup fresh lime juice

2 tablespoons olive oil

2 scallions, diced

2 tablespoons cilantro, chopped

2 cloves of garlic, minced

1 teaspoon cumin

Salt and pepper to taste

For the Jack Cheese sauce:

3 tablespoons butter

3 tablespoon all-purpose flour

2 cups milk

1 teaspoon garlic power

1 teaspoon onion power

1 teaspoon crushed red pepper

1 teaspoon salt

1 teaspoon cracked black pepper

8 ounce pepperjack cheese, shredded

3 tablespoon cilantro, chopped

12 ounces blue corn tortilla chips.

Instructions

Combine all ingredients for the shrimp and allow to marinate for 15–25 minutes. (Do not over-marinate as the shrimp will begin to cook.) To cook, drain the shrimp of its marinade. Heat 1 tablespoon of olive oil in a large skillet. Add shrimp to skillet. Heat until shrimp are pink, approximately 2 minutes per side.

Next, pre-heat oven to 350° Fahrenheit. To make the cheese sauce, melt butter on stove over medium-high heat. Whisk in flour to form a light roux. Slowly stir in milk half a cup at a time, until it forms a slightly thick mix. Mix in garlic & onion power, red pepper, salt, and pepper and whisk until combined. Slowly add shredded cheese until combined and the sauce is smooth. Stir in cilantro until wilted down.

Spread chips over a baking sheet. Heat in oven for 5–7 minutes until chips are warm.

To serve, arrange tortilla chips on a platter. Drizzle cheese over chips. Top with shrimp.

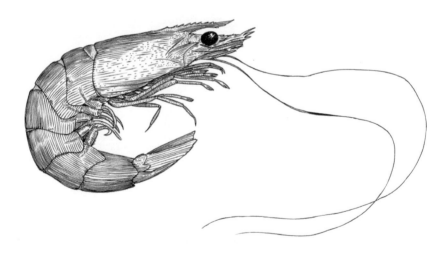

an excerpt from The Abyssians

Lindsay Ahl

> *your face is my chosen abyss*
> —Gwendolyn MacEwen

White tablecloths, Patmos shrimp, white wine, long
      sun through windows, a group
dinner, smart conversation, all beside
           the point as a mania rises
     in my chest, unstoppable.
               Talking casually
to the woman next to me, I slink down
     in my chair: grip your ankle—the only necessity:

if I wasn't touching you
     there would be no way to take my next
breath, no way to live through the next
          moment.

If you are the only one,
     if you were always there—

my ineluctable
     connection
    to the infinite: if every tree, person,
       wall, road, glass—

If—
    I touch you, I touch everything.

Patmos Shrimp

Lindsay Ahl

Ingredients

5 ripe tomatoes
6 tablespoons olive oil
¼ cup chopped onion
½ cup dry white wine
3 tablespoons chopped cilantro (or parsley)
½ teaspoon dry oregano
1 teaspoon salt
3 twists freshly ground pepper
1½ pounds raw shrimp, peeled and deveined
1 teaspoon dried mint
8 ounces feta goat cheese

Instructions

Peel, seed, drain and chop tomatoes. Pour oil in heavy 12-inch skillet and heat over medium flame. Add onions and stir for 4 minutes. Add tomatoes, wine, 1 tablespoon parsley, oregano, salt and pepper. Heat to a boil and cook stirring frequently until mixture softens to puree. Add shrimp and mint and cook 5 minutes.

Stir in 2 ounces of crumbled cheese and sprinkle top with cilantro (or parsley).

Serve with thinly sliced feta, French bread and salad.

Serves 6

Feast

Ruth Bavetta

You are the papaya of my life,
sweet and juicy as August heat.
You are not cool as a salmon
splayed on a plate in the back
of the refrigerator, nor sour
as the lemon in its bright
untruthful skin. You are warm
and sweet, smooth as custard
scented with vanilla. Come
into my kitchen, love,
find the feather bed of good cooking.
Let me be the stocking
on your rolling pin, the slotted spoon
of longing. Together we will find
the measuring cup of desire.

Papaya and Grilled Shrimp Salad

Ruth Bavetta

Ingredients

⅓ cup brown sugar

⅓ cup lime juice

1 cup olive oil

1 hot red chili, chopped fine (adjust amount to get
   desired degree of hotness)

2 cloves garlic

½ cup cilantro, chopped

¼ cup chopped mint

24 large peeled shrimp, tail on, broiled

24 slices ripe papaya

Mixed baby greens

Instructions

Mix first 7 ingredients for dressing. Toss greens with cilantro and mint. Arrange on individual plates. Arrange 4 shrimp and 4 slices of papaya on each plate. Pour dressing over.

Drink to the Animals

Eric Morris

Dearest Beloveds, let us christen our last meal with
punchlines and curse one another for the qualities
of our birthmothers that we see in each other. Raise the faux
crystal and tell yourselves, *Deep breath. Deep breath.*
As you hold the glass, think calm thoughts about
acupuncture and imagine everyone at this table naked.
Let us toast to the fact that we are fully-clothed in our
wingtips and bodices, and give thanks to the creature
that gave itself unto slaughter, our indigestion pending.
Here we drink to the animals who threw themselves
in front of our automobiles. We drink to the life unlived,
the sorrows unsorrowed, the candied yams. Now let us
raise the chalice in moral victory and proclaim the end
to the Battle of Thermopylae. The children up past their
bedtime due to commercial interruption. We thank our God,
the Great Mover, he who giveth and he who taketh away,
for the leftover meatloaf. O the cold heart of some jilted
veggie lover. We drink to those wounded in action, and say,
For a gunshot wound, that's not too bad. Let's drink as lovers
unrequited. You be Juliet and I'll be Raskolnikov. We can bury
the bodies where the dogs sleep. There are so many toasts
that will go untoasted like all the girls never kissed, a maiden
voyage, the captain went down before the ship. Beloveds, take my
hand and bow your heads in prayer. Take my hand and tell me about
your first time. Let us be drunk, speaking of our politics (Marxist),

our religious quandaries (existential), our bodies' inadequacies
(state the obvious). Bow your heads, stare at your crotches, think
about what you've done. *What've you done?* Stormed the beaches
of Normandy? Performed *Hamlet* Off Broadway? Let's drink to forget
the long way home. And eat to remember ourselves as animals on
the verge of eradication. Here's to good food and even better
obituaries. Here's to us, avid golfers, butterfly enthusiasts, mustache
aficionados. Here's to good health and good sex until our eternity
ends, a bridge under construction. Let the alcohol define the symmetry
of our bodies, where one ends like the lakeshore and the other
is a lighthouse lusting for its reflection in the water. Drink, please.

Ribs—Wherein I Frankenstein Recipes Together and Call It My Own

Eric Morris

I understand that Northeast Ohio isn't exactly a BBQ hotbed like Memphis, St. Louis, or, you know, any place south of the Mason-Dixon Line. But like any good American boy, I wanted to try BBQing ribs. And, after weeks obsessing and researching, BBQ them I did. When I finished my rib experiment, I felt like the Greek God of Propane or the Patron Saint of Pork Meat. This feeling, while euphoric, faded fast once I realized the dishes had as much sauce on them as the ribs (I'm a messy cook), but the mess was worth the reward. What follows is the culmination of my recipe browsing and website surfing which resulted in a rib recipe that I call my own.

Ingredients

Two racks of pork ribs (I use spare ribs because they are the cheapest and you can always cook more ribs, grill size depending.)

Yellow Mustard

Dry rub (I use *Finger Lickin' Good* dry rub, but I'm sure most will suffice.)

BBQ Sauce (Again, any brand should work, but I used *Finger Lickin' Good* for consistency.)

A bag of woodchips (I use hickory.)

Twelve pack of beer (I usually go with Labatt Blue or Rolling Rock, but the beer of your choice will certainly work. The beer is not part of the recipe, but for the griller. It's a long process and grilling makes a person thirsty and who BBQs without beer anyway?)

Utensils

Gas or charcoal grill (I recommend using a gas grill, because it's easier to maintain the temperature and you won't have to bother with adding fresh charcoal.)

A good knife

A cutting board

Disposable bread pan (the foil kind)

No stick spray (PAM will work, or you can buy fancier ones.)

Tongs (big tongs)

A brush for the sauce

A nice beer koozie (see above)

Lots of paper towels (this may be obvious)

Instructions

Soak your wood chips (a generous amount). Woodchips + H2O + Tupperware = soaked—nothing fancy there. Take the ribs out their package, admire them, and then rinse them under cold water and pat dry.

Grab your cutting board and knife and trim off any excess fat and skin—the white stuff. You can't miss it. You can also try pulling it off, but depending on the quality of the meat, you may or may not be able to do that.

Spread some yellow mustard over the ribs—not a whole lot but enough to cover them.

Generously apply the dry rub—I apply it to both sides. Let the ribs sit out on the counter for about thirty minutes.

The cooking style is called indirect because, well, the ribs are cooked indirectly, so you only need to heat half of the grill. The ribs will cook on the opposite side of the flame. So while the ribs are hanging out on the counter, start warming up the grill to three-hundred (300) degrees approximately. It's next to impossible to be exact, but at least be in the ballpark, a small ballpark.

As the grill is warming, place the soaked woodchips in the foil bread pan, cover the top with tin foil, and then poke holes in the foil lid. Before you put the ribs on, spray the grill with the no-stick spray. Now you may need to cut the slabs of ribs in thirds or fourths (I know! I know! It sounds blasphemous) in order to fit them on the grill—smaller, thinner pieces of the rib will actually cook on the top rack if your grill has one. If you have a large grill, you can ignore this step and be pleased with your large grill.

Place the woodchip bin on the side of the grill that is on/lit/hot/smoking. Lay the ribs bone-side up on the grill so their u-shape can hold the juices in. Please be certain to lay the ribs on the unlit side of the grill otherwise they will burn. A lot.

Close the grill and, despite temptation, it is ideal for the grill to stay closed for two-and-a-half to three hours—Who am I kidding? It's impossible not to peek, but try to keep it to a minimum.

Crack open a beer, if you haven't already!

After two-and-a-half to three hours of elapsed time (let the trumpets sound!) the ribs should be done. The ribs are done when they fold or start to fall apart when you lift them with your big tongs. Slather them in sauce, lots of sauce, there can never be too much sauce.

Cut, serve, devour.

Celebrate with, you know, a beer or two and then do the dishes.

Meatloaf

Stephen Gibson

No tray should be pulled out of a chiller as if from a morgue,
when all it contains are the ingredients on a sheet for meatloaf.

Meat—milk, garlic, onions, salt, pepper, eggs, bread, parmesan
(& some like raisins)—it's not like it's a feat to make meatloaf.

The course chef was a control freak insisting we had to trim
our bricks, then chill them in pans—it had to be neat meatloaf.

(This woman I cheated with often during the class lent me
a bottle of Tabasco sauce to add a little heat to my meatloaf.)

Ground chuck—when I looked at mine, I saw my mom's hands
decades ago kneading because-she-loved-the-three-of-us meatloaf.

Mary Agnes' Meatloaf

Stephen Gibson

Ingredients

1 ½ to 2 pounds ground chuck

1 large egg

1 medium chopped onion

½ to ¾ cup milk

4 slices white bread, ripped into small pieces

1 teaspoon of minced garlic

Salt and pepper (to taste)

Handful of raisins (optional)

Grated Parmesan (to taste)

Topping (my addition): ½ cup of ketchup and squirt or two of A.1.
  Garlic & Herb Marinade

Instructions

Combine in a bowl and knead ground chuck, egg, onion, garlic, milk, bread, parmesan and raisins. Salt and pepper to taste.

Place into a 5 x 9 inch loaf pan. Spoon ketchup and A.1. Garlic & Herb mix over top of loaf.

Bake at 350° Fahrenheit for about one hour. Let sit a minute.

Serves 6 to 8

Slow-Cooking

Renee Emerson

Outside the sumac limbs sag,
the vow of winter already
weighing.

A late dinner, drowsy, shaping bread
on the baking stone.

Yellow squash, onions, carrots,
a roast and small potatoes
slow-cooking.

My hands bitter with chopped onions,
apron on, the slow-soak of waiting
for you to come home.

My self-reliance, old trophy,
what once carried me,

swallowed
in the night's cataract, the moon,

and stars like small umbrellas,
opening.

Harvest Pot Roast

Renee Emerson

Ingredients

2 yellow squash
3 carrots
3–4 red potatoes
1 white onion
1 garlic clove
5 pounds chuck roast
2 cups beef stock

Instructions

Dice carrots, squash, potatoes and onion and place in crock pot. Pour in the beef stock. Add garlic clove, salt and pepper to taste. Brown the chuck roast in a frying pan for a minute on each side, then add chuck roast to crock pot.

Cook on low for six to eight hours.

Serves 6

Grandmother's Magic Act

Julie Babcock

She gestures over the empty roasting pan.
Dark recessed enamel
pocked with marks where meat
used to cling. She has scraped,
braised, seared and rendered ready.
One wooden spoon—
the magic wand from an Ash tree
split by lightning and gnawed
by black squirrels. Look!
The pan is empty isn't it? Knock
on the bottom. Tap on the sides.
Slip your fingers over the edge.

With this wooden spoon,
a few scrapes, and a watery mist—
Heimlich! There she is young.
There she is walking into her past
where her brother is still alive
laughing with her in this field.
In these mounds of upturned earth
enough potatoes for everyone.

Sunday Pot Roast

Julie Babcock

Ingredients

3 pounds chuck roast
2 tablespoons oil
Salt and pepper, to taste
1 beef bouillon cube
Handful of herbs from the garden, or 2 teaspoons dried
1 pound new potatoes, halved
1 pound carrots, peeled and cut into 2-inch chunks
2 celery ribs, cut into 1-inch chunks
2 onions, quartered
¼ cup flour

Instructions

For the roast, preheat oven to 325° Fahrenheit. Trim fat from meat and brown in hot oil. Place meat in roasting pan. Dissolve bouillon cube in ¾ cup hot water. Add herbs, salt, and pepper to taste. Pour liquid over roast, cover with aluminum foil, and bake 1 hour. Add vegetables, cover, and bake 1 more hour.

For the pan gravy, remove roast and vegetables from pan.

Skim off fat. You should have enough liquid left to make 1 ½ cups. If not, add water.

Stir ½ cup water with ¼ cup flour and add to pan juices. Place pan on medium heat and stir and scrape until thickened.

Serves 6–8

Food for Thought

Lilian Cohen

We raise our glasses for a toast
l'chaim, to life we chorus
then edge to sadness in our thoughts.
We talk about the beauty of her funeral
the eulogies so painfully delivered—
one focused on her love of family
protecting nature and the bush
another on her love of food and wine
another on her belly-laughing humour
despite her rootless troubled youth.

I serve the dishes I'd prepared my guests—
the meat fragrant with Middle Eastern spices
the ratatouille glowing and capsicum scented
the simplicity of white basmati rice.
I savour the blend of flavours and colours
each one uplifting the whole
and think of the textures and hues
of each of the eulogies—
how together they presented a composite richness
a celebration to ease the loss.

Beef and Eggplant Tagine

Lilian Cohen

Ingredients

3 tablespoons olive oil

1 kilogram good stewing beef, diced

2 medium onions, diced

3 cloves garlic, crushed

3 teaspoons ground coriander

1–2 teaspoons each ground ginger, cumin and sweet paprika

¾ cup beef stock

4 medium tomatoes chopped

1–2 eggplants sliced thinly, sprinkled with salt about 20 minutes, rinsed and drained.

Instructions

Heat half the oil in tagine or a large saucepan. Cook beef in batches till browned. Remove.

Sauté onion. Add garlic and spices and cook, stirring, until fragrant.

Return beef to tagine with stock and tomato. Bring to boil, reduce heat and simmer covered about 45 minutes.

Uncover, simmer uncovered about 30 minutes or until beef is tender.

Meanwhile, heat remaining oil in frying pan and cook eggplant about 10 minutes or until tender.

Season to taste. Stir into tagine.

Serves 6

Fit for a King

E.G. Happ & Shirley Chen

I wonder what fits a king—
extra-large?
loud and booming?
pomp and circumstance
with tubas?
but when you placed the lamb shank
on a bed of polenta, mushrooms and greens,
all became clear,
and I felt moved
to make a decree.

Slow Braised Lamb Shank in Shiraz & Rosemary

E.G. Happ & Shirley Chen

Ingredients

Note: The meat needs to be marinated overnight, so please prepare this ahead of time.

For the lamb:

6 lamb shanks—excess fat removed

2 cup of Shiraz

3 stems of fresh rosemary (leaves only)

¼ cup of soy sauce

3 cloves of fresh garlic (cut into slivers)

1 teaspoon of white pepper

1 tablespoon of sugar

For the sauce:

1½ cups of prunes (pits removed)

⅔ cup of Shiraz

1 teaspoon of ginger powder

1 teaspoon of cinnamon powder

Instructions

When you buy the lamb shanks, please make sure you have the bones still attached. This recipe will cook the lamb shank as an entire shank so please tell your butcher not to cut them into smaller pieces. Wash the lamb shanks under cold water and pat them dry. Find a container which is big enough to hold all your lamb shanks during the marinade process. Or you can use a couple ziplock bags.

Mix the Shiraz, soy sauce, rosemary, garlic, white pepper and sugar in a bowl. Make sure the sugar dissolves completely. Pour the marinade into your container (or ziplock bags), and the meat should be submerged in the liquid. Keep this in the fridge overnight.

On the second day, when you're ready to cook the lamb shanks, preheat the oven at 425° Fahrenheit. Arrange the lamb shank as a single layer in a baking dish. (Discard the marinate and remove any remaining rosemary and garlic attached to the meat.) Tightly cover the baking dish with a foil.

Once the oven temperature has reached 425° Fahrenheit , place the lamb shank into the oven and turn down the heat to 300° Fahrenheit immediately. Slowly braise the meat for 2 hours until the meat is almost falling off the bone. Rest the meat for 15–20 minutes before serving.

To prepare the sauce, find a small sauce pan and put all prunes and red wine in. Cook the prunes over medium low heat until soft. About 10 minutes. Season the prunes with ginger and cinnamon. Serve warm or at room temperature.

From Potatoes

Tracy Youngblom

buried like the eggs of extinct species
in warm soil, heavy in the hand as grief,

coated with the dust of their womb:
grace. One hundred twenty-five pounds

per year, every one of us, not for nutrition—
more potassium than a banana, more usable iron

than any vegetable—but for taste, gleam,
white sparks exploding under our forks,

starlight we swallow, other-worldly. Not
always so. The Spaniards who stole them from the Incas

(whose fervor was religious, potato-shaped jugs,
plaques, the tubers used to divine truth,

predict weather) fed them only to peasants
and hospital inmates. Much maligned fruit,

nightshade's cousin, staying underground, blameless—
only the leaves are poison—and patient, yes, patient...

Never bothered by its own dissection, it trusts
the way the soil eases cuts, scars them first, a coating

rough as stone, then braves the sheathing that keeps
the heart unseeing, so it can be renewed. Oh, heart

of wartime sustenance, accepted as payment
by Dutch monks and priests, you grew

in stature because of nobles, Frederick the Great,
who ordered peasants to guard potato fields, threatened

to cut off noses and ears if they refused to eat.
Parmentier, too, set guards over his fields

but dismissed them at night, enticing the French to steal,
plant, eat the fruit on which he had survived

his seven years as prisoner. Marie Antoinette,
known to wear your flowers on her gowns, in her hair,

so adored your sweet sparkle that she rescued you
from suspicions of spreading leprosy, syphilis,

and of causing laziness (not unlike the French court),
while Ben Franklin, visiting then, carried home

an idea that set his brain, but not his country,
on fire. Slow to catch on—seven crossings

before the new America would plant you—
finally goaded on by the Irish, who would know,

their two million escaped, having staked their claim
and failed: 80% of their diet, 10 potatoes per day,

all the plants and a fourth of the population wiped out
by *Phytophthora infestans* and heavy rains.

Oh, Second Bread to the Russians, rugged nugget,
gold to the miners who traded their day's haul

for a couple of spuds—you have been lucky,
and you have been our luck, the luck of chefs who,

catering to their rich clients' whims and tardiness,
discovered french fries and soufflé. And amateur

botanists began to breed you for luscious varieties
we now crave, driven by hunger, that first burst

of hot skin we can't wait to savor. We need them all,
any of the many: tawny russets—the Norgold,

the Ranger, the Krantz—and globular reds—NorDonna,
La Rouge, Sangre, Viking. We are not ashamed.

We love your skin so thin a fingernail can scrape it,
a brush scrub it to edible tatters. You have become

our habit, historical savior, humble fruit we eat
in abundance, you inhabit us. Now, cleansed,

held up by the sink, window high—oh, staunch starch
of our fathers, oh, matter of any meal, embodiment

of multiple economies of the soul—your wet skin,
its tiny field of hairs, moving as weeds on an ocean floor

that wave in the sea's sobbing breath, catches the light
and directs it to us, through you, oh, delivering

in your pure purpose, us, back to our better selves.

Scalloped Potatoes and Pork Chops

Tracy Youngblom

Ingredients

6 pork chops, at least ½ inch thick
2 tablespoons vegetable oil
Salt and pepper
3 tablespoons butter or margarine
3 tablespoons flour
1 ½ teaspoons salt
¼ teaspoon pepper
2 cups chicken broth
6 cups sliced potatoes (peeled or unpeeled)
1 medium onion, sliced thinly, separated into rings

Instructions

Brown pork chops in oil in heavy skillet, then sprinkle with salt and pepper to taste. Set aside. Melt butter in sauce pan. Stir in flour, salt, pepper, and then slowly add broth while stirring. Continue stirring until mixture thickens and boils. Remove from heat.

Place sliced potatoes in greased 9 x 13 pan. Top with onion rings. Pour broth mixture evenly over top. Place pork chops on top of potatoes. Cover pan with foil and bake at 350° Fahrenheit for 1 hour. Uncover and continue baking 30 minutes, or until meat is tender.

Serves 6

Kitchen Histories

Claire Van Winkle

> O good bread,
> When it is given to guests
> With salt and good will!
> —Wesoazjan Kochowski

At the kitchen sink my grandmother
  would suck meat from the turkey's boiled neck
    then turn again to her work—cleaning the headless bird,
      patting it dry, pulling the legs down and back.
        She'd take a length of twine, cinch it
          in her bared teeth, and fasten together the spindly wings.
            Irreverent to recipes she would dash and pinch,
              season to taste. She measured with her eyes.
                She would dig her fingers in for the gizzard—
                  taking care to waste no part of the body—
                    then scrub her hands clean, wringing them,
                      rubbing the goose-flesh skin.

I remember the first time
  you pressed your skin to my skin.
    You took off my glasses, then yours,
      freed my hair and touched my neck.
        You kissed me there. I was thin. The hard floor
          of your mother's kitchen bruised my back,
            but in the din of it all we didn't care.
              My sharp shoulder blades fanned out like wings.

You opened my thighs and spoke softly, in Spanish.
I didn't understand. I just closed my eyes,
pressed my hand flat on the terracotta tile,
and tasted the salt of your body on my body.

Chiles mexicanos range in color, strength,
flavor, size, length, and shape of body;
the *chilhuacle negro* is broad-shouldered
with sweet heat and slick black skin,
while the *cascabel,* or "little rattle",
is brown and dry, with thin skin and a narrow neck.
The thick-fleshed, heart-shaped *poblano* is best "sweated":
oiled, salted, then roasted front and back,
carefully, over low heat. *Arte de la cocina*:
Hot peppers and the firefighting rice that waits in the wings,
ready to play its part in the passion, to soothe
the smiles that burn below bright, tearing eyes.

Near the end, your mother couldn't eat. So small
in her big kitchen, she'd sit through dinner, closing her eyes,
fed by the nearness of the living. By then she'd lost
her strength and the color had gone from her skin.
Now all the things your mind keeps buried are exhumed
by restless senses: the smell of death—her body
wasting through too-sweet perfume. The sound
of her last rattling breath and the sick crack of her neck
when you took her empty body, pulling it from the bed.
Her head—still heavy—rolling, snapping back.
The story written in cursive scars that showed when
her robe slipped, its silk sleeves slack as broken wings.

On the last evening of her life, my grandmother
  ate a small order of White Fence Farm chicken wings
    and an enormous piece of chocolate cake. A true product
      of *kuchnia polska,* in my grandmother's eyes
        a balanced diet was salty, sour, sweet, and rich. *Kielbasa,*
          pickled herring, cherry *pierogi.* Fresh cream. The body,
            she said, was not built for food with too much heat.
              "*Chilly,*" she'd say, "gives such a flush to the skin."
                I remembered this at her wake. Her face was blushed,
                  her lips lined with red. A high collar hid her pale neck.
                    Her glasses had been removed for the viewing.
                      Before they closed the casket, I put them back.

I light the stove to heat tortillas
  while you lie still, peaceful, on your back.
    I almost forget that wars have been fought
      over our families' tables. Loach, snow bunting, waxwing—
        so much of the game is extinct. So much
          of the Deluge gleams in the potato's eye.
            So much is lost between the white flour of my North
              and the rich corn of your South, our continent a broken body.
                So we raise the dead with photographs. We hold down our fort,
                  free and warm within the soft borders of our skin.
                    When you wake we cry over onions, and laugh. We stir
                      and steam. We take a bottle of good red wine by the neck.

Here I am, a baby clinging to my grandma's neck.
  There's you with your mother, a note in her hand on the back.
    We do this often—stay up late in the kitchen, looking through pictures.
      Cooking, talking, remembering. Kissing.
        I say you have her eyes. You say I have your body.
          We share histories that live beneath the skin.

Indyk I Pasilla Gulasz

(Turkey and pasilla stew)

Claire Van Winkle

Ingredients

Turkey

> *traditional/adventurous:* 10–15 turkey necks, cleaned and patted dry
>
> *readily available/easier to handle:* 3 pounds boneless turkey breast, cut into 1-inch cubes

¼ teaspoon salt

¼ teaspoon black pepper, freshly ground

1 cup all-purpose white flour

3 tablespoons vegetable oil

4 garlic cloves, minced

1 large white onion, chopped

3 celery ribs, chopped

2 tablespoons sesame seeds

5 chile pasilla peppers (whole, dried)

> *for mild stew:* chop the peppers into small pieces, removing the seeds
>
> *for a slightly spicy stew:* chop the peppers into small pieces, retaining up to 2 teaspoons of seeds

2 teaspoons adobo de achiote (annatto paste)

2 bay leaves

Mexican oregano—5–7 sprigs fresh, 1 teaspoon dried

2 cup diced tomatoes

2 cups chicken or turkey stock (use stock with low or no salt; the liquid will be reduced, and condensed broths with added salt can overwhelm the dish)

3 cups Spanish yellow rice or white rice

Instructions

Rinse the turkey meat and pat it dry. Combine flour, salt, and pepper in a shallow bowl. Gently roll the turkey in the flour mixture to coat each piece.

Heat the oil in a medium to large stockpot over medium/low heat. Carefully add the turkey pieces. Brown meat on all sides. Remove the meat and set it aside. Add the garlic and onion to the pan drippings and sauté for about two minutes, adding more oil if needed.

Add the celery, sesame seeds, pasilla peppers, adobo de achiote (annatto), bay leaves, and oregano. Stir together. Return the turkey to the pot and mix all ingredients well. Sauté for about two minutes.

Add the stock and diced tomatoes. Raise heat to medium/high and bring the stew to a boil. Reduce heat, cover, and simmer for one hour, stirring occasionally. Reduce the liquid to the consistency of a thick gravy, removing the lid if necessary to speed reduction.

While the stew simmers, prepare the rice. When the stew is reduced and the meat is tender, remove the pot from the heat. Let it sit uncovered for 5 minutes. Serve with rice, garnishing each plate with sesame seeds.

Serves 4–6

Haloing the kitchen table

Jesse DeLong

Haloing the kitchen table, the gaslamp flares on the silverware. Outside, the sun, receding, polishes a spoon on the last lumps of snow.

He can regard all moments as equal and inter-
changeable. So, too, we promised in the straightjacket of time.
Dragging a chicken, squawking, to a stump, I splintered her.
Before the blade, she could regard all moments as equal.
We fried her plucked flesh in lard all winter.
So, too, did the Admiral's mood soften, become brined.
Regarding all moments, he could enter each equally.
The same, though changed. So, too, we promised.

Chicken Noodle Soup with Homemade Egg Noodles

Jesse DeLong

Ingredients

For the soup:
1 ½ shredded cooked chicken breasts
7 cups chicken broth
3 cloves peeled minced garlic
2 teaspoons minced onions
2 celery ribs
2 carrots
Handful of parsley, finely chopped.

For the egg noodles:
2 cups flour
3 egg yolks
1 whole egg
2 teaspoons salt
¼ to ½ cup of water

Instructions

To make the egg noodles, mix flour, egg yolk, whole egg, & salt in a bowl. Add water. Mix with hands. Turn dough onto floured cloth or covered board. Knead until smooth and elastic, about 10 minutes. Cover and let sit for 10 min. Roll dough between ¼ or ⅛ inch thick. Cut into strips size the way you want. Place on paper towel to dry for a couple hours.

After noodles are ready, cut up carrots and celery. Add everything to a crockpot and cook on low for 4 hours.

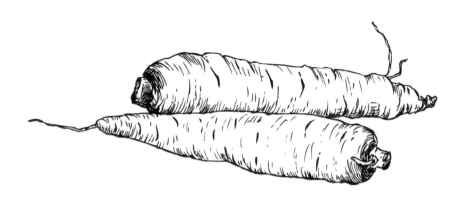

Seven Ways of Looking at a Corkscrew

Tina Schumann

Oh you little purveyor
of necessary violence.
Always drilling towards the sweet stuff.

Domestic augur. Supplier of sin
and swirl—I love you.
I love you because

You make me say the words:
Montalpulciano D'Abruzzio,
Brunello, Barbaresco.

Oh you tool of ancient knowledge,
minimalist of the pull and pop.
Cool and steely under pressure.

Teach me to float above the vine.
Give me reason to be hard.
Train me to lie dormant in a glove box.

Oh you one trick implement,
so happy to oblige.
How have I discarded you?

Took you for a con?
Blamed you for my habit,
and thrown you to the drawer.

Praise be to you and the cork,
a partnership sublime and mature—
adults in an adult situation.

Let's make a bond today;
I will succumb to the juice
and you will mark the way.

Chicken in Wine

Tina Schumann

Ingredients

1 cut up, bone-in, skin-on fryer or fryer parts of choice. (I use one large
  breast cut in half, 3 legs and 3 thighs for four adults.)

2 to 3 tablespoons olive oil or veg oil for sautéing onion and browning
  chicken.

1 medium white onion chopped.

3 cloves garlic, pressed or finely chopped.

1 28-ounce can stewed tomatoes and their juice. (I use cut up tomatoes
  to make it easier.)

1 8-ounce jar drained green olives with pimentos. (You could use green
  Spanish olives cut in half from an olive bar as well.)

3 or 4 sprigs fresh Thyme and two Bay Leaves.

1 bottle white Bordeaux or Pinot Grigio, or any *dry* white wine that you
  like.

1 cup or more chicken stock. (Pan must have enough liquid to cover
  chicken parts.)

Instructions

Salt and pepper generously both sides of chicken parts. Heat oil in a
large Dutch oven or high-sided pot on medium-high heat. Brown chicken
pieces on both sides, about 5 to 7 minutes per side. Remove chicken from
pot and reserve with juices.

Pour in a bit more oil to pot if needed and turn down heat to medium.
Sauté onions and garlic until soft while scraping up brown bits of chicken
fond left in the bottom of pot. Pour in a bit of wine or stock to help with
scraping.

Return chicken to pot. Pour in entire bottle of wine, entire can of tomatoes and herbs. Break up tomatoes with a spoon or crush in hand as they go in *if* you are using whole tomatoes. Check level of liquid. If needed, add chicken stock to cover chicken. Bring to a boil.

Put on lid and turn heat down to a simmer. After about 15 minutes add the olives to the pot. Simmer for another 10 or 15 minutes. Remove skin from chicken pieces and discard. The skin should be soft and pull-away easily from chicken with tongs. Remove bay leaves.

Serve in large soup bowls over rice, boiled egg noodles or boiled potatoes. Crusty French bread is a must.

Note: With leftovers I have been known to remove all bones, shred the chicken meat into smaller pieces, add sautéed sliced crimini mushrooms and/or sliced carrots to make it more of a stew.

With a Smile

Mira Martin-Parker

I work in a room the size of a broom closet and I am happy.
My clothes are full of holes and I am happy.
I eat beans for breakfast and beans for dinner and I am happy.
A pack of peanuts with my paycheck and I am happy.
A 3-cent raise, some personal days and I am truly happy.
I am happy, I am happy
lordy lordy, I am happy
peanuts praises, beans and raises
I am happy.

Boiled Beans

Mira Martin-Parker

Ingredients

2 cups dried pintos, black, or red beans
1 teaspoon dried epazote
1 to 2 dried chipotle peppers
½ teaspoon cumin
Sea salt to taste

Instructions

Rinse beans thoroughly in a colander, checking closely for dirt and stones. Place in glass or ceramic bowl and cover with at least 4 inches of water. Soak overnight. Drain and rinse beans, and place in a large pot.

Cover with about 3 inches of water and bring to a boil. Reduce heat to simmer, and cook for 1½ hours, pouring in additional water as needed. Add dried chipotle peppers, epazote, and cumin and cook until beans are tender. Salt only after beans are completely soft—if you salt too early, the outer skin on the bean will remain hard. To make refried beans, spoon boiled beans into a heated caste iron pan and smash with a fork until smooth.

Cook for 10 to 15 minutes. Serve with steamed short grain brown rice

Deliciousness as a Form of Justice

Laura McCullough

The science of deliciousness reveals a fifth taste—
added to sweet, salty, sour, and bitter—
that thing that might be called fat,
but is closer to protein with the water squeezed out—
      think potato chips or parmesan cheese—
condensation, and the smell—
let's instead say aroma, with its soft three sliding syllables—
all balance and pleasure in the mouth when said aloud like *umami*
and even, that quirky *osmazome*, from the French,
      its Os piggy-backing off the Ms
      and don't you just want to wrap your lips
            around something wonderful?

Is satiety what we all want in the end?
Or will you punish me now for willfulness
      and withholding, your salt in one hand,
      a magician juggling four balls of flavor,
      none sufficient alone, and you thinking,
      what I really need is abstinence, a little
      more time alone with my hungers, and
      then I'll be ready to tell what I know.

Trio of Dishes: A Light Supper

Laura McCullough

Start with red radishes, cut on one end, so they stand nicely, but with their greens left on like tails. Serve on pretty platter with a dish of salt in center. Begin with this to clean mouth.

Offer three pungent small dishes, eat radishes in between as cleanser.

Dish one: one scallop seared and on a bed of arugula, one lemon wedge

Dish two: blue potatoes, cut into halves and sautéed in olive oil. Rosemary sprig on side

Dish three: asparagus, grilled, with butter sauce and ground pepper

Wine as needed.

Dessert

"We dare not trust our wit for making our house
pleasant to our friend, so we buy ice cream."
—Ralph Waldo Emerson

Alchemy

Elizabeth Hilts

Okay, sit back. Get comfortable. I want to tell you a love story.

One pound sweet butter, room temperature.

Your grandmother taught you how to make this shortbread, starting with this: "Darling, let's make some cookies, shall we? Go take a box of butter out of the frigidaire."

Two cups confectioner's sugar.

She did not use confectioner's sugar, she used granulated. If that is what you have on hand, go ahead and use it. The cookies will turn out a little sweeter, the texture more crisp. Shortbread made with confectioner's sugar is a gentler thing, something you learned one day when you'd run out of regular sugar but wanted the comfort of your grandmother's shortbread.

One tablespoon vanilla extract.

You use the double-strength extract made from real vanilla beans from the specialty spice store. One could sip it like a cordial; Grammy would have liked that possibility.

Four cups all-purpose flour.

Unbleached. Organic. Absurd, your grandmother might have thought.

One teaspoon kosher salt. If you use table salt instead, cut it back to half a teaspoon.

"You need the salt to bring out the sweet," Grammy said. Did she even know about kosher salt?

Preheat your oven to three hundred and twenty five degrees. Get out your large baking dish, the one made of Pyrex, the one you thought would be okay for lasagna. Which it is, but it's not *great* for lasagna because that baking dish only holds, what, three or four layers of pasta and meat and cheese at most? That baking dish turned out to be a mistake for lasagna, but it's just right for shortbread.

Now grab that pottery bowl you bought at the Shaker Village in New Hampshire where you and Bernie and Mike spent the day while your husband was at the racetrack. Of course, he wasn't your husband then and you were uncertain if he ever would be. Your grandmother always told you that there are men you should dance with and men you should marry, but she never did explain which was which. That not knowing how you and Neil would end up was one of the things you and Bernie discussed when Mike wandered off to look at the barn or something. That was, in fact, something you and she talked about often. Practically her last words to you in that hospital room were "He'll never give you what you want." How stupid to have been talking about that when there was so much else you wish you'd said, if you had known. But that day, at the Shaker village, she urged patience and you bought this enormous bowl with its two blue stripes.

Put the butter in the bowl and beat it until creamy with a wooden spoon, the way your grandmother taught you. Of course you could do this in a stand mixer, but then you would miss the moment when the butter submits to your touch and begins to transform, going pale and lovely as you marry it to air. Add in the sugar and vanilla, mix well, now add the flour and salt. The dough will be incredibly crumbly, so willfully crumbly that you may doubt that it will ever become anything more than this ragged, unmanageable mess of a thing. But believe me, your faith will be rewarded.

Turn the dough into the pan and press it firmly with your palm until it is evenly distributed. Now take a fork and poke the tines into the dough in as straight lines as you can manage. Place the pan in the oven and bake until the shortbread is firm and lightly browned, about 25 minutes. Your home—this place that your grandmother never saw, that Bernie never saw, this place you share (against all odds) with your husband—will be filled with the aroma of happiness.

Remove the pan and let the shortbread cool for five minutes or so, slice it into small squares and let it cool completely in the pan. Trust me when I tell you that trying to remove the shortbread from the pan before it has set completely will break your heart.

This shortbread is best when it has aged a bit. The cookies soften slightly and the butter, sugar and vanilla settle and merge, the sum of the parts transformed through the everyday alchemy of heat and time. When you pop one of those small squares into your mouth and bite, the cookie will resist for just a moment before it shatters over your tongue into velvet sweet. And you will remember everything that went into its making.

Serves 10

Eating a Herd of Reindeer

Kevin Pilkington

My wife is in the kitchen making
holiday cookies she will place in tins
and send to family and friends.
I walk in to find her humming as she
mixes eggs, sugar and vanilla in a bowl
with a wooden spoon like the one my mother
chased me and my brothers with as kids.

I watch her fill the press with dough
thick as clay then rest the front down
against a pan and clicks the trigger
until there are enough wreaths to hang
on every door in the apartment building.
On top of the oven a tray of stars cools,
an entire galaxy covered in white icing.

She shifts powdered sugar over another
batch on the counter, it falls over them
like a light dusting of snow, that covers
everything but the street. And I enjoy
watching her—maybe it has to do
with the way she measures things
exactly, or how I can always find
a smudge of flour on her neck and forehead.

The world I knew is the one I bolted
the door against every night when I got home.
But this is something I didn't expect, a world
that is as warm as a favorite old sweater
with holes in its elbows. And I can simply
walk into it, open a tin of reindeer cookies,
bite off an antler or two, sit down at the table,
eat a few more, then pour a large glass
of milk to help wash down the entire herd.

Christmas Cream Cheese Cookies

Kevin Pilkington

Ingredients

6 ounces cream cheese—softened

2 cups butter—softened

2 cups sugar

2 eggs

1 teaspoon vanilla extract

1 teaspoon baking soda

5 cups flour

Instructions

Preheat oven—350° Fahrenheit.

Combine the flour and baking soda. In a separate bowl, beat the softened cream cheese and butter until fluffy.

Add sugar, eggs and vanilla. Beat until well mixed.

Add dry ingredients. Mix thoroughly until dough forms.

Insert some dough into cookie press—dough must be at room temperature—press onto ungreased cookie sheets.

Decorate if desired.

Bake for 10 minutes or until slightly browned.

Grandpa Vogt's—1959

Benjamin Vogt

The food is on the table. Turkey tanned
to a cowboy boot luster, potatoes mashed
and mounded in a bowl whose lip is lined
with blue flowers linked by grey vines faded
from washing. Everyone's heads have turned
to elongate the table's view—a last supper twisted
toward a horizon where the Christmas tree, crowned
by a window, sets into itself half inclined.
Each belly cries. Each pair of eyes admonished
by Aunt Photographer. Look up. You're wined
and dined for the older folks who've pined
to see your faces, your lives, lightly framed
in this moment's flash. Parents are moved,
press their children's heads up from the table,
hide their hunger by rubbing lightly wrinkled
hands atop their laps. They'll hold the image
as long as need be, seconds away from grace.

Peppernuts (Pfefferneuse)

Benjamin Vogt

Every Christmas my Mennonite grandmother in Oklahoma would make peppernuts—a very tiny, very crunchy (almost rock hard) cookie that has been made for generations all the way back to Russian and Prussian times; this was a major treat for kids on Christmas morning. Looking back at my life, it was for me, too.

Ingredients

1 cup butter or margarine
4 cups light brown sugar
4 eggs, beaten
1 teaspoon soda in 1 teaspoon hot water
1 teaspoon cinnamon
1 teaspoon ground star anise
½ teaspoon nutmeg
½ teaspoon cloves
7 cups flour

Instructions

Cream sugar and shortening until fluffy. Add eggs, one at a time, beating well. Add other liquids. Sift dry ingredients with spices and flour. Add half amount of flour, mixing well. Add remaining flour and knead well. Store dough in tightly covered container in refrigerator over night or longer.

Roll dough into thin ropes and slice with sharp knife dipped in flour or cold water. Pieces should be about the size of a hazelnut. Place pieces on greased baking sheet.

Bake at 375° Fahrenheit for 7–10 minutes or until golden brown.

New Year's Eve, Seven P.M. EST

Arnold Johnston

Each New Year's Eve at seven, long before
That ball of light brings chaos to Times Square,
And people for whom "Auld Lang Syne's" no more
Than nonsense sing and link hands everywhere,
My wife and I sit quietly and think
Of Hogmanay in Scotland, kith and kin,
And parties past, First Footers coming in
For currant bun or shortbread and a drink,

Whisky for men and sherry for the wives.
We toast our absent friends, eat sweetmeats, too:
I sip on malt, though she prefers champagne.
This moment's pause before our year rings new
At midnight stirs a song and helps maintain
The ties of Auld Lang Syne that link our lives.

Arnie's Scottish Shortbread

Arnold Johnston

Ingredients

2 cups white all-purpose flour, sifted.
1 cup salted butter, softened.
½ cup white granulated sugar.
Optional additions: golden raisins, chocolate chips.

Instructions

Sift the flour into a large bowl; then add the sugar.

If the butter's cold, soften it in a microwave for about 30 seconds at full power. Microwaves vary, so you may need more or less time to soften the butter so it's easy to cream; just remember you don't want it melted.

Using a sturdy wooden spoon, cream the butter in the large bowl with the other ingredients until well combined, but don't overwork.

Now you'll need a standard rectangular metal pan (10 inch x 14 inch); if the pan doesn't have a non-stick surface, use the butter wrappers to grease it.

Press the mixture evenly into the pan. Pierce the entire surface of the mixture with a fork at about ¾"-inch spacing; then use the fork to crimp the edges of the mixture.

To bake, place the pan in an oven pre-heated to 350° Fahrenheit. Bake for about 25 minutes, checking periodically. Not forgetting your oven mitts, remove from the oven when golden brown. Some people prefer their shortbread paler, some more golden brown. You'll find the stage that appeals to your taste, but all the experiments will be delicious.

To cool, set the pan on a cooling rack. After about five minutes, sprinkle the surface lightly with granulated white sugar. After another ten minutes, cut the shortbread into small squares. I generally aim for 35 squares. They're small, but the shortbread is rich—and you can always have another piece! Let cool until crisp. When will that be? You'll probably have to try a few pieces to decide—a tough job, but someone has to do it.

Enjoy! You needn't wait until New Year's Eve, either, and you certainly needn't wash it down with malt scotch or good sherry—but no one's stopping you!

Cold Hands Make the Best Shortbread

Elizabeth Danson

Mama's little children need short'ning bread
she sang in the cold kitchen a fortnight before Christmas
as she mixed the butter, sugar and flour (some had to be
rice flour, a trick she'd learned as a girl in Edinburgh).
Shortbread was extravagant with all that real butter—
Short'ning, short'ning, short'ning, short'ning
a tin of it made a holiday present for friends like
the cobbler down the road who mended all our shoes,
the blind woman who came when she felt lonely,
and helped to polish the silver-plated forks and spoons,
knowing by feel when they were tarnish-free and glossy.
One was sick and the other half dead Mum sang,
mixing in the butter with her always cold fingers
as the five of us watched and listened, hoping for a lick
of the wooden spoon, a scrape of the big yellow bowl.
Mama called the doctor; the doctor said,
Give those children short'ning bread.

Shortbread

Elizabeth Danson

Ingredients

¾ cup all-purpose flour

¼ cup rice flour (Look for it at the health-food store; use regular flour in a pinch.)

¼ cup sugar

½ cup cold butter (If unsalted, add ¼ tsp. salt to the dry ingredients.)

Instructions

Heat oven to 300° Fahrenheit.

Mix flours and sugar together in medium bowl. Grate butter over bowl.

Rub together with fingertips until mixture resembles breadcrumbs (not a dough).

Press down into 8-inch tart pan or pie dish and mark edges with fork tines.

Prick at intervals with fork, and score (not cut) into wedges if desired.

Bake for 40–50 minutes, just until golden brown.

Cool on wire rack for five minutes, then turn out onto bread board.

If scored, break apart into wedges, otherwise (as my Scottish mother did) break into random pieces, "like crazy paving."

Cool completely on wire rack, then store in plastic container (if you must) or biscuit tin (preferably with picture of Queen or Edinburgh Castle on it).

Shortbread will last a week, if not eaten before then.

The Forbidden Fruit

Martha Silano

was probably an apricot
but is almost always depicted

as shiny and red, the tree
the barren woman's supposed

to roll around beneath,
wash her hands with its juice.

How like us to choose,
for our eye-opening snack

the one that hybridizes
with any other *Malus*, so that

planting a seed from a small and sour
might yield a large and sweet.

"A good year for apples,
a good year for twins,"

The Dictionary of Superstitions said,
though weren't we glad when it turned out

not to be true. At the turn of the century,
Tobias Miller brought to Gold Hill, Oregon,

the King, the Northern Spy, the Yellow Transparent,
the Gravenstein, and the Greening,

though we're not sure what we're gathering—
stripey reds we peel and core for sauce,

yellows blushing in the summer sun.
When they ate of it, it tasted good,

twice as good, as say, eternity,
which could not be folded into cake,

which could not be put up or pressed.

Perfect Apple Pie

Martha Silano

Ingredients

6–8 tart apples, pared, cored, and thinly sliced (6 cups)
½–¾ cup white sugar
2 tablespoons white flour
1 teaspoon ground cinnamon
⅛ teaspoon ground nutmeg
Pastry for 2-crust 9-inch pie
2 tablespoons butter

Instructions

If apples lack tartness, sprinkle with about 1 tablespoon lemon juice. Combine ½ cup sugar, flour and spices; mix with apples.

Line 9-inch pie plate with pastry. Fill with apple mixture; dot with butter. Adjust top crust, cutting slits for escape steam; seal. Sprinkle with remaining ¼ cup sugar.

Bake at 400° Fahrenheit degrees for 50 minutes or until done.

Serves 8

To Blueberries

Adele Kenny

Blueberries as big as the end of your thumb,
Real sky-blue, and heavy, and ready to drum
In the cavernous pail of the first one to come!
—Robert Frost, from "Blueberries"

Imagine the *Mona Lisa* with blueberry eyes;
Vincent van Gogh's *Blueberry Night*; imagine
Vermeer's *Girl with a Blueberry Earring* and
Gainsborough's *Blueberry Boy.* Imagine
blueberries, one at a time, between stained fingers—
sugary, tart—large or small (not all created equal).
Full in the sun, even their shadows are warm:
silvery patina, bluer than blue sky, bluer than blue.
First the pop and then pulp between your teeth.
Listen to the birds (sparrows, chickadees)—blue
fruit sweet in their beaks. Oh, briarless bush! Bluest
fruit. No core, no seeds. Nothing ever to pit or peel.
Definitely not the forbidden fruit, no Eve down on
her knees—never the cost of paradise. Blueberry
muffins, pancakes, wine! Highbush and low—blue
on the crest of Blueberry Hill—and years ago, my
mother mixing the dough for blueberry pies, the
rolling pin round in her hands (our dog asleep
on the kitchen stair), my father at the table, and
me on his lap, close in the curve of his arm.

Bluemisu

Adele Kenny

Ingredients

3 pints fresh blueberries (in winter, frozen blueberries may be
   substituted for fresh)
½ cup unrefined sugar
Juice of 1 medium lemon
1 teaspoon lemon zest
1 pint heavy cream
¼ cup powdered sugar
8 ounces mascarpone cheese
12–15 ladyfingers
½ cup of any Raspberry Liquor, Chambord, Crème de Cassis, or
   Crème de Framboise

Instructions

Combine blueberries, unrefined sugar, lemon juice, and lemon zest in
a large saucepan. Bring to a boil over medium heat. Stir to dissolve the
sugar. Reduce heat to medium and simmer for about 5 minutes. Remove
mixture from heat and set aside to cool.

Dip each ladyfinger in whichever liquor you decide to use; be sure to
soak both sides of each ladyfinger (about five seconds on each side). After
dipping, place each ladyfinger on a board to rest while the liquor is infused.

While the ladyfingers rest, combine the heavy cream and confectioner's
sugar. Mix with an electric mixer on low speed until soft peaks form. Fold
in the mascarpone cheese and beat to a creamy consistency at low speed
for about two minutes. (If mascarpone cheese is unavailable, you can cre-

ate a substitute by mixing 8 ounces of cream cheese, ¼ cup of heavy cream, and 2 tablespoons of sour cream.)

Using a large glass compote, make a ring of ladyfingers around the sides and across the bottom of the compote (trim ladyfingers if necessary). Then spoon a layer of mascarpone cream from step 3 onto the ladyfingers. Next add a layer of the blueberry mixture from step 1, and top that with a layer of ladyfingers. Repeat the layering until the compote is filled and your last layer is mascarpone cream. (Alternatively, you might use a rectangular glass baking dish, or individual dishes.) Chill for about four hours. (This dessert keeps well in the refrigerator, so you can prepare it in advance and let it chill overnight.) Just before serving, garnish with fresh blueberries. Other berries can be added to the garnish if you wish (raspberries, blackberries, strawberries). For chocolate lovers, sprinkle unsweetened cocoa powder or bittersweet chocolate shavings on the top layer of mascarpone cream.

Serves 8–10

Blueberrying

Dolores Stewart Riccio

It is the art of knowing that wild
blueberries climb a ravaged hill
where fire took the shade a few years past.
And it is patience for the small blue bells
filling the pail off-key.
                        It is the story
of the sculptor, how she died at eighty-seven
in her kitchen, setting down the strainer
just so no berry spilled, and falling
in her apron out of sight. The sculptor who
was waked with stains still on her fingers.

It is the blueness and the sweetness,
the smell of hot sun and the scratches.
It is her planning to go back next summer,
and our planning. It is remembering our own
good places in the woods.

It is the carefulness of her, as if the woman
bequeathed the blueberries for teacakes to be
served after the funeral. In the presence of
her finished and unfinished work, the taste
of blueberries would nourish our relief
from death.
                        It is to harvest fruit from this

scrub plant that grows best where the pines
were fire-felled and only blackened markers
stand against the sky.
                    It is her resting
after the work. It is dying without
spilling anything, propped up against the sink.

Blueberry Teacake

Dolores Stewart Riccio

Ingredients

1 pint blueberries, picked over and washed

3 ½ cups flour, divided

4 teaspoons baking powder

½ teaspoon salt

½ cup (1 stick) butter, softened

2 cups sugar

2 eggs

1 teaspoon vanilla

1 ½ cups milk

Cinnamon sugar (1 tablespoon sugar mixed with 1 teaspoon cinnamon)

Instructions

Preheat oven to 350° Fahrenheit. Butter and flour, or spray, a 9 x 13 inch pan.

Mix blueberries with ¼ cup of the measured flour. Sift the remaining flour with the baking powder and salt.

Cream butter. Gradually add sugar, then eggs, one at a time. Add the vanilla to the milk.

With beaters on low, add the sifted dry ingredients alternately with the liquid to the creamed mixture, beginning and ending with flour. Fold in blueberries.

Spread the batter in the prepared pan and sprinkle with cinnamon sugar.

Bake on the middle shelf for about 50–55 minutes,until risen, golden, and dry inside when tested with a cake tester.

Serves 12

Pastoral

Brent House

Hunger is a short drive to the old black man who sits & waits.

It's almost all gone.

I'm telling you I saw the man sitting on the roadside & waiting. I'm
telling you there were tomatoes green for frying & plums ripe from the
trees & not much else. It was late in the evening when I stopped.

I'm telling you because I bought the last bag of red tomatoes and a bag
of plums. I paid eight dollars. The tomatoes held the bitterness of red
clay & plums the texture. So good.

I heard the Braves game on his radio.
Jones was at the plate in the top of the eighth.
The Braves were up by three runs.
Smoltz was resting in the bullpen. It was good.

The mafia keeps the Braves from winning all the time so they can make
their money.
They got concessions, he says.

Then, he says, thank you, sir.
& returns me two dollars.

I'll tell you this, ain't nothing more cutting than getting respect you
don't deserve.

It's been a long time since I grown a row of tomatoes.

Then, he tells me he has something to tell me.
Here's the gist of his words:

I have a name.
I believe in God.
God made fruits for us to eat.
I bring those fruits to the roadside.

I am the hand of God.

The gist does not stand for the telling.

I could tell he sold many a load of produce on his telling. The red of his
pickup faded
like the bricks of Sparta; it's so easy to fade. Not so easy to plant &
harvest.

There was music in his telling.
Sure enough the Braves lost to the Giants.
There ain't no way that should have happened.

His telling was poetry I cannot write.

It don't matter though. He's sitting on the roadside just outside Sparta. If
you ask him who he is & what he does

I bet you'll hear the same exact thing I heard.

If you stop by about August I'm told you can get some good
scuppernongs &
muscadine.

Plum Cake

Brent House

Ingredients

2 cups sugar

2 cups self-rising flour

1 teaspoon cinnamon

1 teaspoon ground cloves

½ teaspoon nutmeg

3 eggs

1 cup salad oil

2 jars baby food plums

¾ cup pecans, chopped (optional)

Instructions

Mix dry ingredients first. Then mix eggs, oil, plums and pecans well but do not beat or use an electric mixer.

Bake in greased and floured pan. Bake in tube or flat sheet pan.

Bake in a 350° Fahrenheit oven for 50 minutes or until springy and a toothpick comes out clean.

Use grated rind and strained juice of one lemon with enough confectioner's sugar to make a thin glaze. Pour over cake while warm.

What I Want to Make for You

Natasha Sajé

First I'll find two pears,
green speckled with yellow,
the color of locust trees in May,
two specimens that yield
to slight pressure from my thumb.
They'll sit in the sun, next to an apple
whose ethylene breath will ripen them more,
to the point where even the faintest touch
would bruise them. Then I'll spread out
several leaves of phyllo, sweet
buttering each one with a sable brush,
between whose sheets I'll slip
toasted, slivered, blanched almonds.
I'll cut the pastry into hearts,
one for each of us, baking until crisp—
not long—in the hot oven waiting.
You haven't forgotten the pears?
My knife is so sharp it won't hurt
when I peel and slice them.
More sweet butter and sugar sizzle
in a pan, plus heavy cream,
unctuous, languid, sleepy,
and the pears with some eau de vie,
then a rapid simmer.
Now the assemblage:

One nutty heart on the bottom,
soft sautéed pears in the middle,
another fragile heart on top.
A pool of glossy caramel cream,
also on my fingers with which I offer you
ce mille feuille croquant de poire
au caramel.

Mille-Feuille Croquant de Poire au Caramel

(Crispy Pear Napoleon with Caramel Sauce)

Natasha Sajé

Ingredients

2 sheets phyllo dough

2 tablespoons unsalted butter, melted, plus 1 more tablespoon butter

2 tablespoons sugar

¼ cup sliced almonds

2 Bartlett pears

1 tablespoon brown sugar

¼ cup heavy cream

1 tablespoon pear brandy (eau de vie de poire, sometimes called Williams)

Instructions

Preheat the oven to 350° Fahrenheit.

Place a sheet of phyllo dough on a baking sheet. Brush it lightly with melted butter. Fold it in half and brush it with a bit more butter and sprinkle with sugar and half the sliced almonds. Repeat with the second piece of phyllo and stack the two folded sheets. Brush the top with melted butter and sprinkle with the remaining white sugar.

Cut four three-inch hearts with a cookie cutter, but do not remove the cut-outs from the dough (this will be easier once baked). Bake for 12 to 15 minutes, or until golden brown. Cool and carefully remove the hearts.

Peel and core the pears and slice them thinly. Combine the last tablespoon of butter, the brown sugar and the pears in a saucepan and cook over medium heat until the pears are soft. Let caramelize while tossing, about 10 minutes.

Add the cream and pear brandy and simmer for two minutes. On each of two dessert plates, place a phyllo heart, top with half of the pear slices and cover with another heart. Spoon some sauce around it and serve immediately.

Serves 2

Mardi Gras

Mimi Moriarty

I feel spring in my bones
the winter's core bent
toward the spent sun

the wind slams against
the first day of March
music assails the wreckage

I hear oompah, oompah
the rhythm of Dixie
men in straw hats with horns

my winter self becomes unhinged
the door opens to a festival
filled bowls and loosened buckles

gnomes in the garden
emerging from mounds of snow
trees shaking off their stupor

daughters hover, sons return
the bands, the beads, the coins
the feast before the fasting.

Bananas Foster

Mimi Moriarty

Ingredients

6 bananas
Lemon juice
⅔ cup brown sugar
6 tablespoons butter
Cinnamon
3 tablespoons almond or banana liquor
3 tablespoons light rum
Vanilla ice cream

Instructions

Peel bananas, cut in half lengthwise and crosswise. Brush with lemon juice, set aside.

Melt brown sugar with butter in skillet. Add bananas and sauté lightly until tender, turning once. Sprinkle with cinnamon and liquor. Heat rum separately, pour over bananas. Ignite carefully. After flame goes out, serve over ice cream while still warm.

Serves 6

Pledge

mariana mcdonald

Rice and beans
my days I shall,
gingerbread my nights.

And if I can,
to live I'll flan
the tremors and the fright.

Waiting for *mofongo*,
I hunger at the plate
and reach for taste

my tongue
might waste,
before it is too late.

Mariana's Flan

(with a little help from Francisco)

mariana mcdonald

Ingredients

8 whole eggs
1+ cup sugar
2 cans condensed milk
1 can evaporated milk
1 tablespoon vanilla
2 cups water

Instructions

Preheat oven to 350° Fahrenheit.

First, combine the eggs, slightly beaten, with the condensed milk and evaporated milk. Add water and vanilla. Strain this mixture twice.

Next, caramelize the sugar very slowly until it is completely clear and liquid—it will be a dark brown. Be careful; if the sugar is caramelized too quickly or too long it will burn and be bitter.

Once the sugar is liquid, swirl it onto the inside (bottom and about 2 inches on the sides) of the flan pans. Let the pans cool for a few minutes on racks.

Fill the cake pans with about 1 inch of water. Once the flan pans have cooled, pour the egg mixture into the pans to a height of about 2 to 2½ inches. Then place the flan plans in the water-filled baking pans. (This is what keeps the caramelized sugar from becoming rock candy.)

Place the baking pans with the flan pans "floating" in them in the oven, and cook for about 1 hour to 1 hour 15 minutes, until the tops are golden brown. Take them out and remove the flan pans from the water. Let the flan plans cool for about an hour. Then place the flan pans in the refrigerator overnight.

To serve, let stand at room temperature for a half hour before flipping the flan pan onto a broad, rimmed plate. The best way to do this is to place the plate on top of the flan pan and turn the flan pan over quickly. You may want to slide a knife gently around the top edge of the cooked flan first.

Enjoy!

Serves 8 per flan

Dear as Salt

Ruth Bavetta

on Ralph Going's painting, Double Ketchup, 1996–97

The salt stands iconic on the counter
guardianed by blood-red double ketchups,
flooded with light flowing from the right.

Sodium chloride, a molecule of two,
each harmful alone, when bonded
together they live in harmony.

Halite, hexoctahedral, isometric, perfect
cleavage. Here are pure white cubic crystals
sparkling in a stubby glass shaker

on a diner counter. Sought and sold for seasoning,
medicine, taxes, ketchup, the mining of silver.
Preservative for Egypt's everlasting dead.

The Princess told her father,
you are as dear to me as salt
and he, offended to be compared

to such a commonplace, threatened
to banish her from the palace. Until
she served him roast bream and darioles,

mustard soup, simnel cake, Swithin cream,
pasties filled with marrow, all without salt,
tasteless as a life without love.

Salt makes it harder for things to boil
and harder too, for them to freeze,
prevents the yeast from overflowing.

From mines, from brines, from solar heat,
symbol of fertility, symbol of purity,
regulator of the heart.

Salt is ancient, salt is eternal.
Salt is what he offers me
every night across the table.

Swithin Cream

Ruth Bavetta

(To eat with apple or pear wedges)

Ingredients
2 lemons
8 dandelion flowers
2 cups heavy whipping cream
⅛ teaspoon salt
¾ cup powdered sugar

Ingredients
Grate lemon rind. Chop dandelion petals finely. Mix petals and rind.
Whip cream, adding powdered sugar until thick peaks form.
Fold lemon/petal mix into cream.

In Praise of Consumable Art

Robert Avery

Not those pressed on paper, vinyl, or canvas—
which keep to gather dust—but the one that bears

only an imprimatur of the tongue—
her latest, for example, a chocolate torte

concocted in the common studio
of her kitchen—how she revises an earlier

recipe with ad hoc decisions,
which, like Homer's idylls, are never written

out; how she experiments with a note
of almond or second measure of Chambord,

as Chopin might have tinkered with an étude
never publicly performed; how,

like Pollack with a painting he will slash,
she is suspended above the plate, her poised

spoon drizzling ganache—another fine
confection only the two of us will know,

washed down with the lees of a rare merlot.

Chocolate Torte

Robert Avery

Ingredients

For the sauce:
1 cup fresh black raspberries
¾ cup water
¼ cup honey
1 ounce Chambord (or to taste)
1 teaspoon almond extract

For the torte:
¼ cup black raspberry preserves
2 ounce Chambord
1 cup unsalted butter, cut up
12 ounces bittersweet chocolate
1 ½ cups sugar
6 eggs, at room temperature
¾ cup sifted all-purpose flour
Dash of salt

For the ganache:
1 cup heavy cream
10 oz. bittersweet chocolate (broken)
1–2 oz. Chambord
1 cup toasted sliced almonds, if desired

Instructions

To prepare the sauce, bring water to boil. Stir in honey and raspberries. Reduce heat and boil for 3 minutes. Crush and strain, then add liqueur and extract, and chill.

Next, preheat oven to 350° Fahrenheit. For the torte, butter and flour a 9-inch springform pan and line with parchment. Heat preserves and Chambord to simmering. Mix well and let cool. Melt butter in large saucepan, stirring to prevent burning. Remove from heat and add chocolate. Let stand to allow chocolate to soften. Whisk until smooth. Whisk in sugar, and add eggs, whisking well after each. Whisk in preserves mixture, then blend flour and salt. Transfer batter to lined springform pan and bake on sheet pan approximately 1 hour until cake is puffed and cracked on top and toothpick comes clean. Cool in pan.

To prepare the ganache, bring cream to simmer gently over medium low heat. Remove from heat and add chocolate. Let stand to allow chocolate to soften. Then whisk until smooth. Whisk in liqueur and let glaze stand to thicken.

To assemble, carefully remove cake from pan and invert onto rack. Remove springform bottom and parchment. Place springform bottom on top of cake, then invert cake onto second rack. Pour half of ganache onto cake and smooth over top and side. Refrigerate until set. Repeat with second half of glaze. Sprinkle sliced almonds on top of cake before refrigerating. Cut cake and serve with sauce.

The Best Meal in the History of the World Began…

Amy Lee Scott

With what?

Pomegranate flowers, balsam, the slight singe of ash?
It might have been just the oddest hint of chicory,
Blending with all of the world's unnamed things,
Before minds could dream oceans,
Before lips could psalm hymns.
Indeed, it must have begun before salt,
Before sweet begat sour (or perhaps it did not).

It is known, however, that bittersweet
Did not yet exist between things;
Consequently,
Nor did the suspended delight
Just before glasses clink,
Or when one's skin skims another's
Unexpectedly,
Like dacquoise waltzing on the back of the tongue,
A heedless song rising rich from the belly,
Like loam: *ultima thule*, the damnedest preface.

Hazelnut Dacquoise with Nutella Mousse

Amy Lee Scott

Ingredients

For the Meringues:
2 cups powdered sugar
1 ⅓ cup finely ground hazelnuts
1 ¼ cups finely ground almonds
9 egg whites, room temperature
½ cup granulated sugar

For the Nutella Mousse:
8 ounces cream cheese, room temperature
1 cup powdered sugar
¾ cup Nutella
½ teaspoon vanilla
1 pint heavy whipping cream

To finish:
1 cup sliced, blanched almonds or 2 cups fresh raspberries

Instructions

First prepare the meringues, preheat oven to 275° Fahrenheit. Line two baking sheets with parchment paper and use an 8 inch cake pan to draw three circle templates. Flip the paper over so the written side is face down.

In a mixing bowl, sift together the powdered sugar, ground hazelnuts, and ground almonds. Set mixture aside while you make the meringue.

Put the egg whites in a clean, grease-free bowl. Using a stand mixer or hand mixer, beat the egg whites on low until frothy, about 2 minutes. Increase speed to medium and beat for another 2 minutes, until soft peaks form. Add the granulated sugar and beat for another 2–3 minutes on medium-high, until stiff peaks form. Carefully fold in the powdered sugar/ground nut mixture.

Spoon the meringue into a frosting or plastic zip bag. Cut the tip of the bag and squeeze a spiral circle on the three parchment paper circle templates. Bake for 60–90 minutes, until the meringue is dry. Cool completely on wire racks.

Next, make the nutella mousse. Beat the cream cheese, powdered sugar, and Nutella until well incorporated. Add vanilla. In a separate bowl, whip the heavy whipping cream for 3–4 minutes, until stiff peaks form. Gently fold the whipped cream into the Nutella mixture. Store in the refrigerator until ready to assemble the dacquoise.

To assemble, place the first meringue round on a cake plate. Fill a frosting or plastic bag with Nutella mousse and snip the tip. Squeeze half of the mousse on top of the first meringue. Sprinkle with slivered almonds or fresh raspberries. Repeat with the second meringue round and top the second Nutella mousse layer with the third meringue round. Let the dacquoise sit in the refrigerator for at least 2 hours to come together. Sprinkle with powdered sugar and more slivered almonds or raspberries.

We Catch Her Husband Singing as He Works

Éireann Lorsung

How well we know this lullaby, the one sung
by the pastry chef in his kitchen, where white
light streams in unironically from the Brooklyn
air outside & the late-nineteenth-century
glass continues to flow slowly through its transoms,
the lullaby sometimes whispered under his breath
which smells like chocolate now as he pipes
ganache between layers of tiny, thin wafers, and
sometimes hummed, a sort of ullulating lala
sound he makes when his mind is working on
proportions & his hands are scooping dough
into piles to roll out & press with a circular
or flower-shaped cutter—*that* lullaby, so
familiar, even without words, even in the
bright sun of early spring in the Northern
Hemisphere, undisguisable as a childhood evening
when one parent or another might have taken
each of us upstairs in their arms, singing through
their closed lips the same melody, so that here
in the doorway to this shared kitchen, we can see
once & for all how light surrounds sweetness
& transforms it, making even the unrecognisable
song of someone else's life feel, briefly, like home.

Chocolate Fondant

Éireann Lorsung

Ingredients

3–4 eggs, beaten very well

150 grams butter, cut into small pieces

200 grams good quality, very dark baking chocolate, chopped
   into pieces

100 grams fine white sugar

Instructions

Preheat oven to 375° Fahrenheit

Butter a springform pan and set aside. Beat the eggs very well, until they are quite frothy. The more you beat them, the lighter this (still heavy) cake will be. Set them aside.

While you beat the eggs, melt the chocolate together with the butter in a saucepan (brave) or a bain-marie (safe). Don't let the chocolate burn or clump. Stir well as they melt, and keep from boiling.

Once the butter and chocolate have melted together, remove pan from heat.

Quickly whisk the eggs again, just to reintroduce a bit more air to them, and then add them to the hot chocolate/butter. Immediately whisk together.

This will make a thick, pudding-like mixture. Add the sugar and whisk to combine.

Pour/scrape into pan, and bake to your taste. About 15 minutes will leave a crispy edge and very soft, melting center. Longer will firm up the whole thing to a more brownie-like texture.

Serve with sour fruit (red currants, raspberries) or cream if you're decadent like that.

Note on possible variations: Chili-chocolate fondant: make a simple syrup by boiling sugar and, to your taste, dried red chilis or slices of birds-eye chili. Beat this into the fondant batter just before you add the eggs to replace part of the sugar.

Serves 6

Culinary School

Matthew Gavin Frank

> *"Some cook, some do not cook. Some things cannot be altered."*
> —Dorothy Pound

When gods no longer bow to fresh fruit
(Hanepoot grape, melagrana), the pot
steams away, and we are left dry. This

is the first law of cooking. The second: guesswork
is an accent. It's easy to sandwich bread
with milk, but blood with bandages? What would

the gecko on the wall say? Hovering over Dimitri's
stockpot, the lizard toasts, "*bull*-shit, *bull*-shit,"
from its wealthy throat. Dimitri still wears

Seward's Folly on his sleeve like a thimble,
and the Chef de Cuisine does not appreciate this.
As with any tattoo, it takes more than a toque

to cover it up. Doroteo (this morning, grew
his first moustache, revised the tomato) tells him: to play
with fire is to understand it; a gull in a nest is sunset

between trees and the chimney; scripture was written
by jugglers. The sous chef (hired just last week)
disagrees, thinks of basil as a symphony

without vowels, as decadence in the midst of war.
They all move like greyhounds—buffalo mozzarella
syrup—faster, faster ...

In the walk-in, behind the oxtail stock, Thomas
Edison stands amazed at their fluorescence.

The Revisionist Caprese Salad

Matthew Gavin Frank

Few things (eating notwithstanding) provide greater pleasure than taking an established dish and spinning it, ever so slightly, to the left. The resulting dish will play by the rules of the original, while reinventing itself within these distinct parameters. In this world, what was once an appetizer salad can now be dessert.

Ingredients:

⅓ cup fresh basil leaves

½ teaspoon orange zest

1 cup heavy cream

2 large egg yolks

¼ cup sugar

½ cup finely chopped or shredded fresh buffalo mozzarella, plus 4 thinly sliced discs of buffalo mozzarella, about ¼ inch thick and 2 inches in diameter.

½ cup whole milk

½ cup sugar

1 tomato (heirloom if possible—if not, any good tomato will do), sliced thinly to about ¼-inch thickness.

1 cup tomato simple syrup (recipe follows)

1 cup tomato water (recipe follows)

3 cups sugar

Instructions

For the basil ice cream:

In a small saucepan, combine approximately half the basil, the orange zest, and the cream. Bring to a boil and remove from the heat. Cover and steep for 45 minutes. Using your kitchen facilities, make an ice water bath. You can, quite simply, stop up your kitchen sink, add about 6 inches of cold water (water level will depend on the height of your saucepan—you certainly don't want any water creeping into your ice cream mixture), and a bit of ice.

In a small bowl, beat the egg yolks together with ¼ cup of sugar. After the ice cream mixture has steeped, bring, once again, to a boil. In order to temper the eggs (a process which prevents the eggs from scrambling), very slowly pour in some of the hot cream mixture to the egg bowl, while simultaneously whisking the beaten eggs. Then, pour the tempered eggs from the bowl into the cream saucepan, and cook, stirring often for an additional minute or two, until the mixture coats the back of a spoon. Remove the saucepan from the heat and place in the ice water bath, stirring occasionally, until the mixture is cool. Add the mixture to a food processor and blend thoroughly with the other half of the fresh basil. Strain through a fine-mesh strainer, pour into an ice cream machine, and freeze. Store in an airtight container in the freezer until ready to use. If you have some leftover, it would go perfectly with your forthcoming sweet strawberry ravioli dessert.

For the mozzarella syrup:

Combine the chopped mozzarella, milk, and ½ cup of sugar in a small saucepan and bring slowly to a boil. Remove from the heat and puree the cheese into the liquid with an immersion blender. (If you don't have an immersion blender, add the mixture to a regular blender, puree, and return to the saucepan. Cover the saucepan and steep for 45 minutes. Return the mixture to medium heat and let steam (but not boil) for an additional 3–5 minutes, stirring often. Remove from the heat and strain through a fine mesh strainer. Let cool at room temperature.

For the oven-dried sweet tomato:

Preheat the oven to 275° Fahrenheit degrees. Dip each tomato slice in the tomato simple syrup and place onto a baking rack over a baking sheet pan. Bake in the oven for about 20 minutes, flip the tomatoes and bake for an additional 15 minutes, until the tomatoes have caramelized and dried. Cool at room temperature. Reserve the remaining tomato syrup at room temperature until the dish is plated.

For the tomato rock candy:

In a small saucepan, combine the tomato water and 1½ cups of sugar. Heat over medium-high heat, stirring often, and boil until the sugar dissolves. Add the remaining 1½ cups of sugar and continue to stir until sugar dissolves. Remove from the heat. Let stand for 5 minutes at room temperature, then pour the mixture into a large sturdy drinking glass or glass jar. Meanwhile, tie a few lengths of string along a pencil. The string should be about ½ the height of the glass or jar. Balance the pencil over the mouth of the glass or jar so the ends of the strings hang in the mixture. Allow to sit at room temperature for at least 24 hours or up to a week (the longer you wait, the larger the rock candy crystals). Strip the crystals from the strings. If you have more than you can use for this recipe, save for a late night indulgence.

To make the tomato simple syrup:

Combine 1 cup tomato water with 1 cup sugar (or, in other words, equal parts sugar and tomato water, depending on the yield you desire). Stir. Bring to a boil in a medium saucepan, remove from the heat, and let stand at room temperature until cool. Store the leftover syrup in the refrigerator.

To make the tomato water:

For approximately 2 cups of tomato water, puree about 10–15 good large tomatoes in a food processor with a small pinch of salt. Spoon the puree into an adequately sized piece of cheesecloth and tie it up. Suspend a strainer over a large bowl, place the tied-up cheesecloth into the strainer and set in the refrigerator overnight, or until the juice has dripped from the tomatoes into the bowl. You can save the tomato solids for a home-made vegetable stock. Store the tomato water in the refrigerator (it should keep for about a week, but the leftovers can be frozen).

Plating:
Dip each slice of buffalo mozzarella into the tomato syrup. Place a slice at the center of each plate. With a small ice cream scoop, place a sphere of basil ice cream on top of the mozzarella slice (the scoop of ice cream should just cover the mozzarella). Top the basil ice cream with a slice of oven-dried sweet tomato. Spoon a small amount of mozzarella syrup around the plate. Float a few crystals of the tomato rock candy in the syrup.

Eating:
Ahhhhhhhhhhhhhh. Revisionism.

"After a good dinner one can forgive
anybody, even one's own relatives."
—Oscar Wilde

Acknowledgments

Grateful acknowledgement is made to the editors of the following magazines in which these poems first appeared—sometimes in slightly different versions—and to the authors for contributing their work to this anthology.

The Abyssians (an excerpt), by Lindsay Ahl. Printed by permission of the author.

The Kitchen Weeps Onion, by James Arthur. Copyright © 2012 by James Arthur. First published in *Charms Against Lightning*. Reprinted by permission of the author.

In Praise of Consumable Art, by Robert Avery. Printed by permission of the author. "Chocolate Torte" recipe adapted from *Bon Appétit*, December 2003

Grandmother's Magic Act, by Julie Babcock. Printed by permission of the author.

When Cabbage is Not a Vegetable, by Michele Battiste. Printed by permission of the author.

Feast, by Ruth Bavetta. Printed by permission of the author.

Ode to Sardines, by Ruth Bavetta. Copyright © 2014 by Ruth Bavetta. First published in *Embers on the Stairs* (Moon Tide Press). Reprinted by permission of the author.

Dear as Salt by Ruth Bavetta. Copyright © 2013 by Ruth Bavetta. First published in *Fugitive Pigments* (FutureCycle Press). Reprinted by permission of the author.

Waldorf Salad, by Amy Berkowitz. Printed by permission of the author.

At the End of a Busy Day, by Emily K. Bright. Printed by permission of the author.

Food for Thought, by Lilian Cohen. Printed by permission of the author.

Peaches, by Barbara Crooker. Copyright © 2007 by Barbara Crooker. First published in *Concho River Review*. Reprinted by permission of the author.

Cold Hands…, by Elizabeth Danson. Printed by permission of the author.

Haloing the kitchen table, by Jesse DeLong. Printed by permission of the author.

Blueberrying, by Dolores Stewart Riccio. Copyright © 1987 by Dolores Stewart Riccio. First published in *Ball State Teachers Forum*. Reprinted by permission of the author. "Blueberry Teacake" recipe is a Dolores original from *The Energy Crunch Cookbook* (Chilton Book Company, 1979) by Joan Bingham and Dolores Riccio.

Cabbage, A Love Song; The History of Brussels Sprouts; The History of Watermelon; The History of the Radish, by Marcela Sulak. Copyright © 2010 by Marcela Sulak. First published in *Immigrant* (Black Lawrence Press). Reprinted by permission of the author.

Before Making a Toast, by Marjorie Thomsen. Printed by permission of the author.

Cheers on the Cobblestones, by John J. Trause. Printed by permission of the author.

Kitchen Histories; Amuse-bouche, by Claire Van Winkle. Printed by permission of the author.

Grandpa Vogt's 1959, by Benjamin Vogt. Copyright © 2012 by Benjamin Vogt. First published in *Afterimage*. Reprinted by permission of the author.

Eat Stone and Go On; Sangria & Ceviche, Santiago's Bodega, Key West, Florida, by Joe Wilkins. Printed by permission of the author.

Fruit, by Laura Madeline Wiseman. Copyright © 2014 by Laura Madeline Wiseman. First published in *Some Fatal Effects of Curiosity and Disobedience* (Lavender Ink, 2014). Reprinted by permission of the author.

I Serve It Forth, by Sarah Yasin. Printed by permission of the author.

From Potatoes, by Tracy Youngblom. Printed by permission of the author.

Diane and Anneli would like to offer many thanks to the following people:
To Michele Battiste and Abayomi Animashaun for reading the wonderful deluge of submissions as well as offering creative input on *Feast*.
To Amy Freels, our designer, for making this poetry cookbook as beautiful as we hoped it would be.
To all of the Contributors, for your poetry and recipes: without you there would be no *Feast*.

Author Biographies

Lindsay Ahl's chapbook, *The Abyssians*, was a finalist for the 2013 National Poetry Chapbook Award. Her poetry can be found in the 6th annual *Nazim Hikmet Festival Chapbook, RHINO, The Patterson Review, Vellum, Drunken Boat, New Delta Review*, and many others. Her fiction includes a novel, *Desire*, out with Coffee House Press, and stories in *The Brooklyn Rail, BOMB Magazine, Fiction magazine*, and others. She publishes *Shadowgraph* (www.shadowgraphmagazine.com), an arts & culture journal.

James Arthur's poems have appeared in *The New Yorker, The New York Review of Books, The New Republic, Poetry*, and *The American Poetry Review*. He has received the Amy Lowell Travelling Poetry Scholarship, a Stegner Fellowship, a Hodder Fellowship, a Discovery/*The Nation* Prize, and a residency at the Amy Clampitt House. His first book, *Charms Against Lightning*, was published by Copper Canyon Press in 2012 as a Lannan Literary Selection. James grew up in Toronto and now lives in Baltimore, where he teaches in the Writing Seminars at Johns Hopkins University.

Robert Avery writes and teaches in Bucks County, Pennsylvania. His poems have appeared in a number of journals including *The Southern Review, Mid-American Review, Poetry East*, and *Measure*.

Julie Babcock is the author of the poetry collection *Autoplay* (Nov. 2014) from MG Press. Her poetry and fiction recently appear in various journals including *The Rumpus, Western Humanities Review, Weave*, and *decomP*. She is a recipient of grants and fellowships from the Indiana Artist Commission and the Vermont Studio Center, and she teaches at the University of Michigan.

Michele Battiste is the author of two poetry collections: *Ink for an Odd Cartography* (2009) and *Uprising* (2013), both from Black Lawrence Press. She is also the author of four chapbooks, the most recent of which is *Lineage* (Binge Press, 2012). Her poems have appeared in journals and magazines such as *American Poetry Review, Beloit Poetry Review, Anti-, The Awl*, and *Verse Daily*, and her reviews have appeared in *Rain Taxi,Open Letters Monthly*, and *Rattle*. She has received grants, awards, and residencies from The Center for the American West, AWP, the

Jerome Foundation, the New York Foundation for the Arts, the Poetry Society of Virginia, and the Blue Mountain Center. Michele has taught creative writing and literature at Wichita State University, the University of Colorado, and Gotham Writers Workshop in New York City, but she currently raises funds for nonprofits undoing corporate evil.

Ruth Bavetta's poems have been published in *Rattle, Nimrod, Tar River Review, North American Review, Spillway, Hanging Loose, Rhino, Poetry East,* and *Poetry New Zealand,* among others, and are included in the anthologies *Twelve Los Angeles Poets* and *Wait a Minute: I Have to Take off My Bra.* She has published two books, *Fugitive Pigments* and *Embers on the Stairs.* A third book, *No Longer at this Address,* will appear in 2014. She loves the light on November afternoons, the smell of the ocean, a warm back to curl against in bed. She hates pretense, fundamentalism and sauerkraut.

Amy Berkowitz is the author of *Listen to Her Heart* (Spooky Girlfriend, 2012) and *Lonely Toast* (what to us press, 2010). Her third publication, *Tender Points,* will be published by Timeless, Infinite Light later this year. She lives in San Francisco, where she is the editor of Mondo Bummer Books.

Emily K. Bright holds an MFA in poetry from the University of Minnesota. Her chapbook *Glances Back* was published by Pudding House Press, and her individual poems have appeared in such literary journals and anthologies as *Other Voices International,Gastronomica, North American Review,* and *The Pedestal Magazine.* Follow her commentary on writing and social justice at http://emilykbright.blogspot.com.

Shirley Chen is a committed foodie who has a deep interest in local and seasonal ingredients. She blends Asian influence into her cuisine and is known for experimenting new recipes for dinner parties. As a marketing and strategy consultant, cooking is her oasis for Zen moments of inspiration. Shirley currently lives in Nyon, Switzerland.

Born in Melbourne, Australia, **Lilian Cohen** moved to Haifa, Israel with her husband in 1968 and apart from sojourns in London, Boston and Melbourne, lived there until 2013. She has now returned to Melbourne on a permanent basis. Until her retirement she worked as an English teacher at the Leo Baeck Senior High School in Haifa. She is a member of the Haifa chapter of the 'Voices' poetry association and recently completed a Diploma of Professional Writing and Editing in Australia. Her poetry and short stories have been published in journals in Australia, England, Israel and the U.S., and she has completed a crime novel set in Israel.

Barbara Crooker's work has appeared in journals such as: *The Green Mountains Review, Nimrod, The Denver Quarterly, Natural Bridge, The Beloit Poetry Journal, Poetry International, The Valparaiso Poetry Review, South Carolina Review, Tar River Review, The Hollins Critic* and anthologies, such as: *The Bedford Introduction to Literature, Thirteen Ways of Looking at a Poem* (Wendy Bishop, editor), *Worlds in Our Words: Contemporary American Women Writers* (Prentice Hall), *Good Poems for Hard Times* and *Good Poems, American Life* (Garrison Keillor, editor). Mr. Keillor has read her work nineteen times on *The Writer's Almanac*, and she's been fortunate to receive poetry writing fellowships from the Virginia Center for the Creative Arts; the Moulin á Nef, Auvillar, France; The Tyrone Guthrie Centre, Annaghmakerrig, Ireland; and the Pennsylvania Council on the Arts.

Elizabeth (Mimi) Danson is a long-term member of the U.S. 1 Poets' Cooperative—a weekly workshop for poets of Central New Jersey, which publishes *U.S. 1 Worksheets*. Her writing has appeared there and in other literary journals, including *Slant, The New Yorker, Anon One,* and *Fourth Genre*. Her book *The Luxury of Obstacles* was published by The Ragged Sky Press.

A graduate of the University of Alabama's MFA program, **Jesse DeLong** has found homes for his writing in *Best New Poets 2011, Colorado Review, Mid-American Review, American Letters and Commentary, Indiana Review, Painted Bride Quarterly,* and elsewhere. His chapbook, *Tearings, and Other Poems,* was released by Curly Head Press. "Haloing the kitchen table" is from his manuscript, *Screel*.

Juditha Dowd's poetry has recently appeared in *Cider Press Review, Kestrel, Ruminate, Spillway* and elsewhere. She is the author of three chapbooks. *Mango in Winter,* a full-length poetry collection, was published in 2013 by Grayson Books.

Renee Emerson earned her MFA in poetry from Boston University. She recently published her first book of poetry, *Keeping Me Still* (Winter Goose Publishing, 2014), and her poetry has been published in *32 Poems, Christianity and Literature, Indiana Review,* and elsewhere. Renee teaches at Shorter University in Rome, Georgia, where she lives in a little brick house in the woods with her husband and daughters.

Matthew Gavin Frank is the author of the nonfiction books, *Preparing the Ghost: An Essay Concerning the Giant Squid and Its First Photographer, Pot Farm,* and *Barolo,* the poetry books, *The Morrow Plots, Warranty in Zulu,* and *Sagittarius*

Agitprop, and two chapbooks. His essay collection/cookbook, *The Mad Feast: An Ecstatic Tour Through America's Food*, is forthcoming November 2015 from W.W. Norton: Liveright. Recent work appears in *The Kenyon Review*, *The Normal School*, *The Iowa Review*, *Conjunctions*, and elsewhere. He teaches at Northern Michigan University, where he is the Nonfiction and Hybrid Editor of Passages North. This winter, he tempered his gin with two droplets (per 750ml) of tincture of odiferous whitefish liver. For health.

Stephen Gibson is the author of five poetry collections, *Rorschach Art Too* (2014 Donald Justice Prize, West Chester University), *Paradise* (University of Arkansas Press, Miller Williams finalist selection, 2011), *Frescoes* (Lost Horse Press book prize, 2009), *Masaccio's Expulsion* (MARGIE/Intuit House book prize, 2008), and *Rorschach Art* (Red Hen Press, 2001).

Diane Goettel is the Executive Editor of Black Lawrence Press. She has lived in Hong Kong since 2009. There, she teaches English and writing to non-native speaking children. Diane and her husband Noah are proud parents of a rescue Doberman Pinscher named Spoon.

Karen Greenbaum-Maya, retired clinical psychologist, German major, two-time Pushcart nominee and occasional photographer, no longer lives for Art, but still thinks about it a lot. She started trying to cook when she was six, out of hunger and in self-defense. She has developed professional recipes. For five years, she reviewed restaurants for the *Claremont Courier*, sometimes in heroic couplets, sometimes in anapest, sometimes imitating Hemingway. "Real Poem" received Honorable Mention in the 2013 Muriel Craft Bailey Memorial Competition, and "The poem is a space casual" received Honorable Mention in Found Poetry's 2013 inaugural Dog-Ear Poetry contest. Kattywompus Press published her two chapbooks, *Burrowing Song* and *Eggs Satori*. She lives in Claremont, California. Find links to work online at: www.cloudslikemountains.blogspot.com/.

Ed Happ has been writing poetry for over forty years, often under the *nom de plume* of Gordon Edwards. He is the founder and editor of "The Fairfield Review," Connecticut's first online literary journal. As in poetry, he believes food and wine has something that connects with our own history, and it holds the promise of something more that is 'enclothed' beneath the common surface. Ed is a nonprofit executive living in Nyon, Switzerland.

Elizabeth Hilts earned her MFA in Creative Writing at Fairfield University. Formerly the editor of an alternative newsweekly and editorial director for direct mail companies, she is the author of four humor books and is an adjunct professor of English. Hilts is currently working on a novel and a series of essays. Her work has appeared in *Spry Literary Journal, Extract(s)*, and *Fourth Genre.*

Lynn Hoffman has been a merchant seaman, teacher, chef and cab driver. He's published three novels, *The Bachelor's Cat, Philadelphia Personal* and *bang-BANG*. He's also written *The New Short Course in Wine* and *The Short Course in Beer*. Skyhorse Books just published a second, expanded edition of the beer book. A few years ago, he started writing poetry. In 2011 his poem, "The Would-be Lepidopterist" was nominated for a Pushcart Prize. His memoir of a funny year with cancer, *Radiation Days* will be published in March 2014. Most of the time he just loafs and fishes.

Brent House, a contributing editor for *The Tusculum Review* and co-editor of *The Gulf Stream: Poems of the Gulf Coast*, is a native of Hancock County, Mississippi. His poetry collection, *The Saw Year Prophecies*, was published by Slash Pine Press.

M.J. Iuppa lives on a small farm near the shores of Lake Ontario. For the past ten years, she and her husband Peter Tonery have been committed to food sustainability. She has numerous publications (poetry, fiction, nonfiction and plays) in national and international journals as well as two full length poetry collections *Night Traveler* (Foothills, 2003) and *Within Reach* (Cherry Grove Collection, 2010) and five chapbooks; her latest prose chapbook is *Between Worlds* (Foothills, 2013). She served as the poetry adviser (2007–2012) for the New York Foundation for the Arts, and since 1986, has worked as a teaching artist in the schools, K-12 for a variety of agencies (RCSD, BOCES 2, Young Audiences, Genesee Valley BOCES, Project U.N.I.Q.U.E. and V.I.T.A.L. Writers & Books, and others). Currently she is Director of the Visual and Performing Arts Minor Program at St. John Fisher College.

Arnold Johnston lives in Kalamazoo and South Haven, MI. His plays, and others written in collaboration with his wife, Deborah Ann Percy, have won awards, production, and publication across the country. His poetry, fiction, non-fiction, and translations have appeared widely in literary journals and anthologies. His books include two poetry chapbooks—*Sonnets: Signs and Portents* and *What the Earth Taught Us*—*The Witching Voice: A Play about Robert Burns; Of Earth and Darkness: The Novels of William Golding;* and *The Witching Voice: A Novel from the Life of Robert Burns*. His translations of Jacques Brel's songs have appeared in numerous musical revues nationwide (including the acclaimed Chicago productions *Jacques Brel: Songs of Love and War* and *Jacques Brel's Lonesome Losers of the Night*), and are also featured on his CD, *Jacques Brel: I'm Here!* Commissioned by the Kalamazoo Civic Theatre, Arnie and Debby's interactive drama *The Night Before Christmas* had its highly successful world premiere in December 2012. The New Vic Theatre premiered their chilling comedy, *Giving Up the Ghosts*, in October, 2013. A performer-singer, Arnie has played many solo concerts and some 100 roles on stage, screen, and radio; he has also done individual dialect coaching and group workshops in a range of accents. He is a member of the Dramatists Guild, The Playwrights' Center, Theatre Communications Group, and the American Literary Translators Association. He was chairman of the English Department (1997–2007) and taught creative writing for many years at Western Michigan University. He is now a full-time writer.

Diane Kendig is author of four chapbooks, most recently *The Places We Find Ourselves*. Her writing has appeared in many current journals, such as *J Journal, Wordgathering, New Verse News,* and *qarrtsiluni,* as well as the anthologies *Broken Land: Poems of Brooklyn* and *Those Winter Sundays: Female Academics and their Working-Class Parents.* A recipient of two Ohio Arts Council Fellowships in Poetry, Diane was born and raised in Canton, Ohio where she returned in 2011 after decades away. She lives there in her childhood home with her partner Paul Beauvais and their Scottie, Robbie Burns Beaudig. Find her at her website dianekendig.com or her blog, *Home Again,* http://dianekendig.blogspot.com/

Adele Kenny is the author of twenty-three books (poetry & nonfiction) with poems published in journals worldwide, as well as in books and anthologies from Crown, Tuttle, Shambhala, and McGraw-Hill. A former creative writing professor, she is founding director of the Carriage House Poetry Series and poetry editor of *Tiferet.* Among other awards, she has received two poetry fellowships from the NJ State Arts Council and the 2012 International Book Award for Poetry. www.adelekenny.com

Kathleen Kirk is the poetry editor for *Escape Into Life.* She is the author of six poetry chapbooks, including *Interior Sculpture: poems in the voice of Camille Claudel,* a set of poems commissioned by Columbus Dance Theatre for the world premier of *Claudel,* a dance based on the life and work of the French sculptor. Her work appears in a variety of print and online journals, including *A-Minor, Eclectica, Nimrod, Poems & Plays, Poetry East,* and *Waccamaw.* She lives in Illinois, the Land of Lincoln, and writes scripts for Illinois Voices Theatre. She blogs at http://kathleenkirkpoetry.blogspot.com.

Éireann Lorsung's books are *Music For Landing Planes By* (Milkweed 2007), *Her Book* (Milkweed 2013), and *Sweetbriar* (dancing girl press, 2013). Recent poems appear in *Beloit Poetry Journal, Colorado Review,* and *Women's Studies Quarterly*; excerpts from a novel-in-progress are in *Two Serious Ladies, DIAGRAM,* and *Bluestem.* She runs MIEL, a micropress (miel-books.com).

Mira Martin-Parker earned an MFA in creative writing at San Francisco State University. Her work has appeared in various publications, including the *Istanbul Literary Review, North Dakota Quarterly, Mythium,* and *Zyzzyva.* Her collection of short stories, *The Carpet Merchant's Daughter,* won the 2013 *Five [Quarterly]* e-chapbook competition.

Anneli Matheson is an Associate Editor with Black Lawrence Press. She holds an MFA in Creative Writing from City University in Hong Kong, and worked on *Feast: Poetry & Recipes for a Full Seating at Dinner* while living in Hong Kong, Madrid, Vermont, and Colorado. Her essays have recently appeared in *Cha: An Asian Literary Journal, 5x5 Literary Magazine,* and *Lowestoft Chronicle.* Anneli lives in Boston.

Laura McCullough's books of poetry include *Rigger Death & Hoist Another* (Black Lawrence Press), *Panic* (winner of the Kinereth Gensler Award, Alice James Books), *Speech Acts* (Black Lawrence Press), and *What Men Want* (XOXOX Books), and her first book, *The Dancing Bear* (Open Book Press). Her chapbooks include *Women & Other Hostages* (Gob Pile Poetry Series, Amsterdam Books), and *Elephant Anger,* online at Mudlark. She is the editor of two anthologies, *The Room & the World: Essays on the poet Stephen Dunn* (Syracuse University Presso and *A Sense of Regard: Essays on Poetry and Race* (University of Georgia Press). She is the editor of *Mead: the Magazine of Literature and Libations* and an editor at large for *TranStudies Magazine.* She holds an MFA from Goddard College, and her essays, criticism, poems, creative non-fiction, and short fiction have appeared in or are forthcoming in *The Georgia Review, The Birmingham Review, The Florida Review, New South, Guernica, The American Poetry Review, Green Mountains Review, Pank, The Writer's Chronicle, Gulf Coast, Pedestal, Painted Bride Quarterly,* and many others. She has recently completed a full length memoir, *The Belt of Venus.*

mariana mcdonald's poetry has appeared in *Fables of the Eco-Future, The Southern Poetry Anthology: Georgia, Sugar Mule, Southern Women's Review, From a Bend in the River: 100 New Orleans Poets,* and *El Boletín Nacional.* She lives in Atlanta, where she works as a public health scientist. She became a Fellow of Georgia's Hambidge Arts Center in 2012.

Claire McQuerry's poems and essays have appeared in *American Literary Review, Mid-American Review, Louisville Review, Creative Nonfiction,* and others. Her poetry collection *Lacemakers* won the Crab Orchard First Book Award, and she has been the recipient of a Walter E. Dakin Fellowship and a Dorothy Sargent Rosenberg prize. She is currently a visiting professor at Gonzaga University.

Mimi Moriarty is a poet living in the Hudson Valley of New York State. She has two chapbooks published by Finishing Line Press: *War Psalm,* which came out in 2007, and *Sibling Reverie,* co-authored with her brother, Frank Desiderio, published in the spring of 2012. A third chapbook, *Crows Calling,* was recently published by Foothills Publishing.

Eric Morris teaches creative writing at Cleveland State University and serves as a poetry editor for *Barn Owl Review.* His work has appeared or is forthcoming in *The National Poetry Review, Heavy Feather Review, Dressing Room Poetry Journal, Whiskey Island, The South Dakota Review, Puerto del Sol, The Laurel Review, Pank, Post Road, Thrush, The Jet Fuel Review, The Collagist, Anti-, Devil's Lake,* and others. He lives and writes in Akron, OH.

Robby Nadler did his culinary training at the Le Petit Outre boulangerie and patisserie in Missoula, Montana. He graduated magna cum laude in day breads with minors in night mix and Robyn dance parties. He is ever grateful to Selden, Leif, and the rest of the staff for all they taught him.

Loretta Oleck is a poet and psychotherapist. Her poetry has been published or is forthcoming in *Word Riot, Feminist Studies, The Mom Egg, High Coupe, The Westchester Review, Laughing Earth, Poetica Magazine, Still Point Arts Quarterly, St. Somewhere, Marco Polo Arts Magazine,* among numerous others. Her work has been performed at *The Hudson Valley Center for Contemporary Art,* as well as at other venues in and around New York. She holds a Masters degree in Creative Writing from New York University.

Daniel A. Olivas is the author of seven books including the award-winning novel, *The Book of Want* (University of Arizona Press). He is the editor of *Latinos in Lotusland: An Anthology of Contemporary Southern California Literature* (Bilingual Press), and his writing has been widely anthologized including in *Sudden Fiction Latino* (W. W. Norton), *Mamas and Papas* (City Works Press), and *New California Writing 2012* (Heyday Books). He has written for *The New York Times,* the *Los Angeles Times,* the *El Paso Times,* the *Los Angeles Review of Books, La Bloga,* and other publications. His fiction, non-fiction and poetry have appeared in many literary journals including *Exquisite Corpse, New Madrid, PALABRA, The Pacific Review,* and *The MacGuffin.*

Susanne Paola Antonetta's most recent book, *Make Me a Mother,* was published by W.W. Norton. She is also author of *Body Toxic, A Mind Apart,* the novella *Stolen Moments,* and four books of poetry. Awards for her poetry and prose include a *New York Times* Notable Book, an American Book Award, a Library Journal Best Science book of the year, a Lenore Marshall Award finalist, a Pushcart prize, and others. Her essays and poems have appeared in *The New York Times, The Washington Post, Orion, The New Republic* and many anthologies. She lives in Bellingham, Washington, with her husband and son.

Daniele Pantano is a Swiss poet, translator, critic, and editor born of Sicilian and German parentage in Langenthal (Canton of Berne). His individual poems, essays, and reviews, as well as his translations from the German by Friedrich Dürrenmatt, Georg Trakl, and Robert Walser, have appeared or are forthcoming in numerous magazines, journals, and anthologies worldwide, including *Absinthe: New European Writing, The Baltimore Review, The Cortland Review, Conjunctions, Gradiva: International Journal of Italian Poetry, Guernica Magazine, Italian Americana, Jacket, The Mailer Review, Poetry Salzburg Review, Versal,* and *Verse Daily.* Pantano's poetry has been translated into several languages, including German, Albanian, Bulgarian, Kurdish, and Farsi. Pantano has taught at the University of South Florida and served as the Visiting Poet-in-Residence at Florida Southern College. He divides his time between Switzerland, the United States, and England, where he's Reader in Poetry and Literary Translation at Edge Hill University. For more information, please visit www.danielepantano.ch.

Kevin Pilkington is a member of the writing faculty at Sarah Lawrence College. He is the author of six collections: his collection *Spare Change* was the La Jolla Poets Press National Book Award winner and his chapbook won the Ledge Poetry Prize. His collection entitled *Ready to Eat the Sky* was a finalist for an Independent Publishers Books Award. A collection entitled *In the Eyes of a Dog* was published in September 2009 and won the 2011 New York Book Festival Award. Another collection entitled *The Unemployed Man Who Became a Tree* was recently published by Black Lawrence Press. His poetry has appeared in many anthologies including *Birthday Poems: A Celebration, Western Wind,* and *Contemporary Poetry of New England.* Over the years, he has been nominated for four Pushcarts and has appeared in *Verse Daily.* His poems and reviews have appeared in numerous magazines including: *The Harvard Review, Poetry, Ploughshares, Iowa Review,*

Boston Review, Yankee, Hayden's Ferry, Columbia, North American Review, etc. His debut novel entitled *Summer Shares* was published in June 2012.

Anne Posten writes short fiction and translates contemporary literature from German. Her work has appeared in *FIELD, Words Without Borders, -ality journal, Stonecutter Journal*, and Hanging Loose Press. She was born in Annapolis, MD, and currently lives in Queens, NY.

Yelizaveta P. Renfro is the author of a collection of essays, *Xylotheque*, available from the University of New Mexico Press, and a collection of short stories, *A Catalogue of Everything in the World*, winner of the St. Lawrence Book Award. Her fiction and nonfiction have appeared in *Glimmer Train Stories, North American Review, Colorado Review, Alaska Quarterly Review, South Dakota Review, Witness, Reader's Digest, Blue Mesa Review, Parcel, Adanna, Fourth River, Bayou Magazine, Untamed Ink, So to Speak*, and elsewhere. She holds an MFA from George Mason University and a Ph.D. in English from the University of Nebraska. She currently lives in Connecticut. To learn more about her work, visit her blog at http://chasingsamaras.blogspot.com/p/writing.html.

Natasha Sajé is the author of three books of poems, *Red Under the Skin* (Pittsburgh, 1994), *Bend* (Tupelo Press, 2004), and *Vivarium* (Tupelo, 2014); a book of poetry criticism, *Windows and Doors: A Poet Reads Literary Theory*, (University of Michigan Press, 2014); and many other essays. Her work has been honored with the Robert Winner and Alice Fay di Castagnola Awards, a Fulbright fellowship, the Campbell Corner Poetry Prize, and the Utah Book Award. Sajé is a professor of English at Westminster College in Salt Lake City, and a member of poetry faculty at the Vermont College of Fine Arts M.F.A. in Writing Program.

Tina Schumann's manuscript *As If* (Split Oak Press) was awarded the Stephen Dunn Poetry Prize for 2010. Her work has been a finalist in the *National Poetry Series*, the *Four Way Books Intro Prize* and the *Terrain.org* poetry contest. She is the recipient of the American Poet Prize and received honorable mentions in *The Atlantic* and *Crab Creek Review* poetry contests. "Seven Ways of Looking at a Corkscrew" was nominated for a Pushcart. She is editor of the forthcoming anthology *Two-Countries: U.S. Daughters and Sons of Immigrant Parents*. Her work has appeared in various journals and anthologies including *The American Poetry Journal, Ascent, Cimarron Review, Harpur Palate, Nimrod, PALABRA, PARABOLA, Poemeleon, Poetry International, San Pedro River Review, Terrain. org, Raven Chronicles* and *The Yale Journal for Humanities in Medicine*. Please visit www.tinaschumann.com to learn more.

Amy Lee Scott received an MFA from the University of Iowa's Nonfiction Writing Program. Her essays have appeared in, or are forthcoming in, *South Dakota Review, Bellingham Review, Gettysburg Review, Michigan Quarterly Review, Gulf Coast, The Southern Review, New Letters, Fourth Genre, Brevity*, and others. Her writing has been on the notable list in *The Best America Essays 2009* and reprinted in Dzanc Book's *Best of the Web 2010* and Bedford/St. Martin's *The Practice of Creative Writing, 2nd ed.* She blogs about food, travel, and books at clubnarwhal.blogspot.com.

Vivian Shipley is the CSU Distinguished Professor and teaches at SCSU. Her ninth book, *The Poet*, was published in 2015 by Louisiana Literature Press at SLU. *Perennial*, her tenth book, is forthcoming in 2015 from Negative Capability Press at University of South Alabama. Other poetry awards include the Lucille Medwick Prize from the Poetry Society of America, the Robert Frost Foundation Poetry Prize, the Ann Stanford Poetry Prize from the University of Southern California, the Marble Faun Poetry Prize from the William Faulkner Society, the Daniel Varoujan Prize from the New England Poetry Club and the Hart Crane Prize from Kent State. Raised in Kentucky, with a PhD from Vanderbilt, she was inducted into the University of Kentucky Hall of Distinguished Alumni in April, 2010 and was awarded a CT Arts Grant for Poetry in 2011. She lives in North Haven, CT with her husband, Ed Harris.

Leah Shlachter's poems have appeared in *Bamboo Ridge* and *The Owen Wister Review*. She is a Kundiman fellow and has also received support from the Wyoming Arts Council. She is currently working towards her MFA in poetry at Pacific University. She lives in Jackson, Wyoming.

Martha Silano is the author of four books of poetry, including *The Little Office of the Immaculate Conception* and *House of Mystery*, both published by Saturnalia Books. She teaches at Bellevue College.

Erin Elizabeth Smith is the Creative Director at the Sundress Academy for the Arts and the author of two full-length collections, *The Fear of Being Found* (Three Candles Press, 2008) and *The Naming of Strays* (Gold Wake Press, 2011). Her poems have appeared in numerous journals, including *Mid-American, 32 Poems, Zone 3, Gargoyle, Tusculum Review,* and *Crab Orchard Review*. She teaches a bit of everything in the English Department at the University of Tennessee and serves as the managing editor of Sundress Publications and *Stirring*.

Sheila Squillante is the author of the poetry collection, *Beautiful Nerve*, as well as three chapbooks of poetry. Her poems and essays have appeared widely in print and online journals like *Brevity, The Rumpus, Phoebe, Cream City Review, South Dakota Review, Quarterly West, Literary Mama, Glamour Magazine* and elsewhere. She is associate director of the MFA programs at Chatham University in Pittsburgh, editor-in-chief of *The Fourth River* literary journal, and associate editor at *[PANK]*.

Dolores Stewart Riccio's poetry has appeared in *The American Scholar, Atlanta Review, Bellowing Ark, The Beloit Poetry Journal, Chicago Review, Connecticut Review, Denver Quarterly, The Deronda Review, Fiddlehead, Poetry, Quercus Review, Salmagundi, Southern Poetry Review,* and other journals. Two collections of her poems *Doors to the Universe* and *The Nature of Things* have been published by Bellowing Ark Press. As Dolores Riccio, she has authored several cookbooks, most notably *Superfoods: 300 Recipes for Foods that Heal Body and Mind,* (Warner Books, 1992).

Marcela Sulak is the author of *Decency* (BLP, 2015) and *Immigrant* (BLP, 2010) and the chapbook *Of all the things that don't exist, I love you best.* She's translated four collections of poetry from Israel, the Czech Republic and the Democratic Republic of the Congo, and she's co-edited *Family Resemblance: An Anthology and Exploration of Eight Literary Hybrid Genres* (Rose Metal Press, 2015). She directs the Shaindy Rudoff Graduate Program in Creative Writing at Bar-Ilan University, is an editor at *The Ilanot Review* and *Tupelo Quartery*, and hosts the TLV.1 Radio podcast *Israel in Translation.*

Marjorie Thomsen holds an MSW from Catholic University. She won the New England Poetry Club's 2012 Firman Houghton Award. Her poem, "Rondeau for My Grandmother" was a finalist in the 2014 Common Good Books/Love Poem contest judged by Garrison Keillor, Tom Hennen and Patricia Hampl. Her poems have been published in a variety of literary journals including *Mobius: The Journal of Social Change, Poetica Magazine* and *Haibun Today.* Her first poetry collection, "Pretty Things Please" will be published in 2016 (WordTech Communications/ Turning Point). She grew up in Richmond, Virginia and currently lives in Cambridge, Massachusetts.

John J. Trause, the Director of Oradell Public Library, is the author of *Eye Candy for Andy: 13 Most Beautiful ... Poems for Andy Warhol's Screen Tests* (Finishing Line Press, 2013); *Inside Out, Upside Down, and Round and Round* (Nirala Publications, 2012); the chapbook *Seriously Serial* (Poets Wear Prada, 2007; rev. ed. 2014); and

Latter-Day Litany (Éditions élastiques, 1996), the latter staged Off-Off Broadway. His translations, poetry, and visual work appear internationally in many journals and anthologies, including the artists' periodical *Crossings*, the Dada journal *Maintenant*, the journal *Offerta Speciale*, the Uphook Press anthologies *Hell Strung and Crooked* and *-gape-seed-*, and the Great Weather for Media anthology *It's Animal but Merciful*. He has shared the stage with Steven Van Zandt, Anne Waldman, Karen Finley, and Jerome Rothenberg, the page with Lita Hornick, William Carlos Williams, Woody Allen, Ted Kooser, and Pope John Paul II, and the cage with the Cumaean Sibyl, Ezra Pound, Hannibal Lector, Andrei Chikatilo, and George "The Animal" Steele. He is a founder of the William Carlos Williams Poetry Cooperative in Rutherford, N. J., and the former host and curator of its monthly reading series. He has been nominated for the Pushcart Prize (2009–2011, 2013).

Claire Van Winkle received her BA from New York University and her MFA in Poetry Writing and Literary Translation from Queens College of the City University of New York. In addition to her creative endeavors, Claire works as a recreational therapist at the New York State Psychiatric Institute where she explores the writing workshop as an element of therapy. Claire's work has been honored with the Lenore Lipstein Memorial Poetry Award, a Hunter College Memoir Prize, the Mary M. Fay Poetry Award, and an Academy of American Poets Prize. She currently teaches at Queens College.

Benjamin Vogt is the author of the poetry collection *Afterimage* (SFA Press, 2012) and two memoirs. He has a Ph.D. from the University of Nebraska–Lincoln and an M.F.A. from The Ohio State University. His nonfiction, poetry, and photography have appeared in *Creative Nonfiction, Orion, Subtropics, The Sun*, and several anthologies including *The Tallgrass Prairie Reader* (Iowa, 2014). Benjamin lives in Lincoln where he freelances as a garden writer and owns a prairie landscape consulting business, while teaching English at the University of Nebraska.

Joe Wilkins is the author of a memoir, *The Mountain and the Fathers: Growing up on the Big Dry* (Counterpoint 2012), a 2012 Montana Book Award Honor Book and a finalist for the 2013 Orion Book Award, and two collections of poems, *Notes from the Journey Westward* (White Pine Press 2012), winner of the 17th Annual White Pine Press Poetry Prize, and *Killing the Murnion Dogs* (Black Lawrence Press 2012), a finalist for the Paterson Poetry Prize and the High Plains Book Award. A National Magazine Award finalist and PEN Center USA Award finalist, his poems, essays, and stories have appeared in *The Georgia Review, The Southern Review, Harvard Review, Ecotone, The Sun, Orion*, and *Slate*, among other magazines and literary journals. Of Wilkins' work, Deborah Kim, editor at the *Indiana Review*, writes, "The most striking component of it is its awareness of 'the whole world.' What is ordinary becomes transcendent. In places derelict and seemingly unexceptional, Wilkins compels us to recognize what is worth salvage, worth praise." Though born and raised on the high plains of eastern Montana, Wilkins now lives with his wife, son, and daughter in western Oregon, where he teaches writing at Linfield College. You can find him online at http://joewilkins.org/.

Laura Madeline Wiseman is the author of over twenty books and chapbooks and the editor of *Women Write Resistance: Poets Resist Gender Violence* (Hyacinth Girl Press). Her recent books are *Drink* (BlazeVOX Books), *Wake* (Aldrich Press), *Some Fatal Effects of Curiosity and Disobedience* (Lavender Ink), and the collaborative book *The Hunger of the Cheeky Sisters* (Les Femmes Folles) with artist Lauren Rinaldi. Her work has appeared or is forthcoming in *Prairie Schooner, Margie, Mid-American Review, The Iowa Review, Calyx, Ploughshares,* and *Feminist Studies*. Currently, she teaches English and Women's and Gender Studies at the University of Nebraska-Lincoln. www.lauramadelinewiseman.com.

Originally from the idyllic coast of Maine, **Sarah Yasin** presently lives inland where she studies world literature in translation using the public library. She teaches Latin at a private high school and moonlights at the checkout counter of a convenience store. She is a Municipal Liaison for National Novel Writing Month, and a facilitator for writing retreats in New Hampshire. Her recent or forthcoming poems can be found in *J Journal, Gravel,* and *Pirene's Fountain*.

Tracy Youngblom earned an MA in English and an MFA in Poetry from Warren Wilson College. Her first full-length collection of poems, *Growing Big,* will be published in September 2013 by North Star Press. Her chapbook of poems, *Driving to Heaven,* was published in 2010 (Parallel Press) and was reviewed in *The Georgia Review*. Individual poems, stories, and book reviews have appeared or are forthcoming in journals including *Shenandoah, New York Quarterly, Briar Cliff Review, New Hibernia Review, Slate, North Stone Review, Aethlon, Potomac Review, Poetry East, Ruminate, Weave magazine, Emprise Review, Frostwriting,* and others. She teaches English full time at Anoka-Ramsey Community College, lives with her husband and dog, and spends as much time as possible with her three grown sons.

Black Lawrence Press would like to cordially invite you to share your feast with us!

Dear Reader,

We invite you to host a party, cook up a recipe or two from *Feast*, read a poem and toast aloud, and then share your event with your fellow readers and eaters!

Please visit the *Feast: Poetry & Recipes for a Full Seating at Dinner* Facebook page (facebook.com/FeastAnthology) for more details and information.